GO
BACK,
YOU
DIDN'T
SAY
"MAY I"

THE
DIARY
OF
A YOUNG
PRIEST

Thomas
Jackson

GO BACK, YOU DIDN'T SAY "MAY I"

A Crossroad Book
THE SEABURY PRESS | New York

The Seabury Press
815 Second Avenue
New York, New York 10017

Copyright © 1974 by The Seabury Press
Designed by STAN DRATE
Printed in the United States of America

Grateful acknowledgement is made to Harcourt Brace Jovanovich, Inc. for
permission to reprint the excerpts from "The Little Prince" by Antoine
de Saint-Exupery; and to *Ramparts* magazine for permission to reprint the
excerpt from "A Devout Meditation in Memory of Adolph Eichmann" by
Thomas Merton.

LIBRARY OF CONGRESS CATALOGING IN PUBLICATION DATA

Jackson, Thomas, 1942–
  Go back, you didn't say "May I".

  "A Crossroad book."
  1. Jackson, Thomas, 1942–   I. Title.
BX5995.J23A33   283'.092'4 [B]   74–11382
ISBN 0–8164–1170–0

Preface

This subjective, personal journal is part of a larger volume which I prepared for our children: Jennifer, Peter, and Lisa. Over the past few years, as I attempted to find the particulars of my own father's life, it occurred to me that I might provide some material for our children; perhaps in future years, as they face the joys and sorrows and ambiguities of their own lives, they may want to know what we were trying to do in *these* bizarre times.

I have chosen to alter a few names and dates to protect the lives of specific persons, and these should be obvious to the reader. And, in most instances, I have not included the pedantic *sic* to note errors by other writers; the documents are generally printed as written originally.

Apologies are due. Given the limitations of time, space, and personal perception, I have undoubtedly omitted thousands of names and incidents. My lack of omniscience is obvious, but I here note the community of people in my life, whether recorded or not.

I extend deep thanks to patient and helpful typists—Rosie Wood and Barbara Moote—and to diligent and expressive proofreaders—Lee and Barbie Worman and Grace Gerbrandt. And thanks to Paul and Kate for their coffee, their living room, and their friendship near the waterfall.

670737

Finally, I recognize the vanity, the embarrassment, and the risk in a personal history.

So be it.

Peace.

Thomas Jackson

Ithaca, New York
February, 1974

To Judith

Whose gentleness and laughter and understanding allow my secrets of the heart and give others the freedom to speak.

GO
BACK,
YOU
DIDN'T
SAY
"MAY I"

I

"You do not live here," said the fox. "What is it that you are looking for?"

"I am looking for men," said the little prince.

"Men," said the fox. "They have guns, and they hunt. It is very disturbing. They also raise chickens. These are their only interests. Are you looking for chickens?"

"No," said the little prince. "I am looking for friends. What does that mean—'tame'?"

"It is an act too often neglected," said the fox. "It means to establish ties."

" 'To establish ties'?"

"Just that," said the fox. "To me, you are still nothing more than a little boy who is just like a hundred thousand other little boys. And I have no need of you. And you, on your part, have no need of me. To you, I am nothing more than a fox like a hundred thousand other foxes. But if you tame me, then we shall need other other. To me, you will be unique in all the world. To you, I shall be unique in all the world. . . ."

—Antoine de Saint-Exupéry,
The Little Prince

August 15, 1969

We are here.

The new co-director of the United Campus Ministry at Ohio University has arrived in Athens, Ohio, with his wife and two weary kids.

We're in a new home, surrounded by endless pyramids of

I

yellow packing boxes, by scurrying carpenters, spattered painters, serious plumbers, and shouting electricians, each with a dozen questions about color, location, size, and alternatives.

There were no parades or banners or fireworks as we drove in but *we are here*. The present tense of that statement speaks a satisfaction only imagined during these last three months of upset and chaos. What a very long road we traveled to get here, what a refuge for the spirits this large, old house seems to afford!

Just five years ago, Judy and I were riding in my parents' new '64 Lincoln, traveling from the Detroit airport to their suburban home. Christmas snow, a school vacation, the warmth of the car and of my family's greetings, the satisfaction of our first full year of marriage—all of these things provided the setting I needed to make my announcement.

For the past eighteen months, I had played musical vocation in my head: whenever the academic melody stops, switch to a different vocational decision. Why not become a doctor? Architect? How about the law? Ever think of social work? Give business a try so you can take over your father's corporation. Hey, journalism is your interest, right?

Judy had listened to it all amid family, friends, and university counselors. And always she said, "Tom, you could do any of those things, but do what you want to do."

As the car sped toward that home of memories, I nervously made my announcement: "Dad, mom, I've decided something. For a variety of known and unknown reasons, I'm applying to an Episcopal seminary. I want to try it for a year, just to see what happens. I don't know what to expect really, but I have to try it."

My father rarely took his eyes off the road when he drove, but he quickly glanced at me, and at mom and Jude in the rearview mirror—and he smiled broadly.

A few of the windows are now bracing air conditioners, so the humidity seems less an enemy to our homesteading chores. Jenny is searching each corner of each room for her elusive toy box. Peter, whom we received from the New York adoption agency only two months ago when he was four months old, is probably wondering if this crazy, nomadic Jackson family has finally found a permanent home. And I wonder with him. We *all* wonder and hope.

My parents' home in the Detroit suburbs was our home, too, for the summer of '66, as I did some intern work for the Episcopal parish next door.

On April 3, my father had died, weakened by two years of hospitals and killed by two months of leukemia.

In May, I had been elected president of my class in seminary, an event of surprise and needed support.

In June, two letters arrived. The one from seminary informed me that my candidacy for Holy Orders was being denied, for I didn't seem to be an "asset" to the seminary. The second letter, from a classmate who was several years older than I, said that he was willing to help me fight the decision, that he could not return to seminary if I was being tossed out. A virtual stranger had never before made a commitment to me like that.

As I ran a few errands this afternoon, I seemed to notice a genuine friendliness in the faces and voices of these Athenians. It's a Norman Rockwell kind of town. Some farmers casually look at machinery in front of a feed store. A bearded professor gazes through a bookstore window. An Appalachian mother shops and copes with three crying toddlers. Four long-haired men in tank shirts play a lazy game of touch football. A clothing merchant laughs with a passerby in front of his store.

*The fires around our parish in Detroit during the civil re-
volt of '67 had tempered some of our hopes, but also offered
a quick education for our partial naïveté. Those fires of frustration and destruction also focused some light on the desperate
needs of the people in the ghetto—and on the characters of
those involved.*

"Okay, Mac, how many grenades you got stashed in there,"
the cop demanded as he pulled me out of my Volkswagen at
a roadblock.
"I'm sorry, Father," another officer immediately added, "but
the sergeant's a bit uptight with all of this gunfire going on."

Our street seems almost pastoral. Each side is lined by
gigantic maple trees, creating a tunnel effect from one end to
the other. Punctuations of sunlight mark the shadowed side-
walks here and there.

The driveway is composed of bricks bearing the "Athens"
seal, separating our house from that of the Charles', a family
with six active and gentle children. Oddly enough, the youngest
is a recently adopted biracial son, as our son Peter is. It seems
like an incredible coincidence, but one which symbolizes our
present feeling of finding a good home for all of us in so many
ways. Maybe that driveway doesn't separate but connects!

*I sat alone in the huge hall of the New Jersey parish on that
May evening a few months ago, feeling like Jonah inside the
whale. I had been asked to leave my ministry in the parish two
weeks before. Now I waited while the rector and the vestry—a
jury of twelve—voted on my petition to have parish support for
a street ministry in the area.*

*As I sat on the slightly elevated stage, staring down at the
richly tiled floor, I tried to sort out the bizarre and overwhelming events of that day. I still wasn't sure about the nature of my*

shortcomings, nor why I expected a favorable decision on my petition.

Now and then I could hear the drone of discussion from the next room, followed by sudden, prolonged periods of laughter.

Why are they laughing?

There had been extensive arguments and debates in the parish during the preceding days; many people seemed pleased with my apparent departure, while others were extremely upset about it. Various parishioners had various reasons for wherever they stood.

I felt betrayed and partially destroyed.

More laughter. Why?

About noon on this day, Jude received a call from the adoption agency, informing us that they had a son for us. Amid despair, we rejoiced.

What can they be saying about me to cause such laughter to reverberate through this empty hall?

Later in the afternoon, Jude got a long-distance call from Chicago: her brother had received a grenade wound in Vietnam.

And now this debacle tonight.

An endless day. Too many emotions, too many people in too many places defining our fate.

The laughter ended abruptly. I sat in silence. The door opened. The group entered the hall, some eyes on me, some eyes searching the same slick tile. I was called to the rector's office and given the official decision.

"You are to cease your ministry in this parish and this community immediately. You are to vacate the house as soon as possible. You may return to the parish building to move your personal property from the office." Etcetera.

I went home in a deeper despair than I had ever known, to try to explain to Jude what I did not understand; to tell her that our five thousand dollars used to improve the house was

*apparently down the drain; to tell her that we had to leave very
soon; to talk with her about her brother and our new son; to
tell her, amidst my own uncertainty, that we would surely find
another job somewhere; to tell her that we could go up to our
small farm in New York until something came along; to tell
her hopes which I didn't have; to tell her of my deep love for
her.*

Why on earth were they laughing?

And now we are here. A complicated nine-year trip, full of
magnificent roadside rests and ghastly potholes. The last two
stops were planned to be about four years each, but things
turned out differently.

Now, I'm painting walls in a new home in a new town for a
new job. And I hope it's four-year paint.

August 16

Believe it or not, I left the door unlocked last night, and
not one thing was stolen! Incredible. No one in Athens has
double and triple locks on their doors. People walk on the
streets at night and don't look terrified of each other. Haven't
they experienced Chicago, Washington, Detroit, Manhattan,
and all points east and west? Was it simply first-night luck, or
is this summary, student-vacant town one of those places you
read about in *The New York Times,* where the crime wave
hasn't broken the dike? I had thought that such places were
make-believe.

August 18

A large envelope arrived in the forwarded mail today, con-
taining two complimentary copies of the September issue of

The Episcopalian magazine. The lead photo-article deals with the experimental liturgy we did in the Jersey parish several months ago, before I had even the slightest hint that my days were numbered.

There I stand on the chancel steps, leading the packed house in a celebration of life, looking as nervous and pleased as I felt that day, hoping that the success of that liturgy would motivate the parish into new areas of liturgical expression. But knowing that it probably wouldn't.

It was a good day, though, and I thought that my relationship with the rector was reciprocally strong. I thought that any disagreements with the more conservative members could be worked out in one way or another. I thought wrong.

I think about the whole thing too much. I've got to get this hostility out of my system, and quit portraying myself as some sort of tragic figure in my fantasies. But it was like a huge divorce, and I constantly think of what might have been.

The large picture of me in the magazine was taken just at the moment when I was nervously moistening my lips, and consequently the tip of my tongue protrudes from my mouth. It looks as though I'm sticking out my tongue at the whole parish. Good grief.

August 21

The week has been full of busy work at U.C.M. (United Campus Ministry), trying to get my office in order, my head oriented. I've had several meetings with Tom Niccolls, the other co-director, and Don Craig, a minister and doctoral candidate in counseling, who is working part-time this year on a special project.

After the experience in Jersey, I have become too sensitive about co-workers: I look them over carefully, trying to find out immediately what they *really* expect of me, and acting rather paranoid about the working relationships. I've got to get over that.

Both men seem to be magnificent human beings.

Tom Niccolls has been here since '58, I guess, first as a Presbyterian chaplain to students, working out of this place (then known as the Westminster House) and the local parish. We seem to complement each other in several ways: he is taller, quieter, and older than I. In his late thirties, with a brush cut, he emits a security and trustfulness which is apparent at once. He listens intently, responding with the steady enthusiasm and sincerity which alleviate my own suspicions. He seeks my friendship by allowing me to accept his.

I want to hear his stories of these past eleven years, the stories of battles won and lost, the stories which have surely engraved the deep but gentle lines of his gaunt face. I want to be a part of the new stories.

Don Craig is also a Presbyterian minister, but doesn't emphasize it much, knowing that the minister tag can be a bit of a hang-up in the university corridors. His gregariousness and empathy radiate rather than overwhelm, and the animation of his face and laughter put me at ease.

Earlier this week, together with a few other campus ministers, we met with the newly appointed vice-president for Educational Services, considered sort of the number-two man in the administration of the new university president, Claude Sowle. This man, Richard Dorf, came here a couple of months ago to be the dean of Engineering, and within a few weeks was appointed to this post. The shelves in his rather swanky office were lined with engineering books today, and he seemed a bit harried by the sudden shift in job description.

It was one of those very polite meetings in which we talked little, but rather listened to his views on the campus ministry.

"I would hope that you gentlemen can act as a bridge between the students and administration," Dorf concluded with certainty and smoothness.

"A bridge sometimes gets walked on from both ends," Niccolls quipped. Amid various knowing smiles and assurances of mutual aid, the meeting ended.

August 23

The "bridge" blew up today. And I can't get over it.

Last night, the city and county police, together with men from the prosecutor's office and the state investigative agency, carried out a series of drug raids.

Twenty-six people, mostly students, were arrested, in the largest drug bust in Ohio in a long time. Some people came to see me at the house this afternoon, asking me to go to the jail to see the prisoners, to check on them, to find out if they were all right.

Twenty-one of them are now in jail, and I understand that the local judge, Franklin Sheeter, has set bond at five thousand dollars per person, with a general charge of "possession of marijuana." My visitors, who seemed very straight (including one young university administrator) contended that there really wasn't any evidence on most of the prisoners and that the warrants were totally illegal. They tried to tell me of a history of bad relations between students and the police (they mentioned especially a police captain named Charles Cochran) but, in the too-animated discussion, I was confused by the inundating particulars. I decided, though, to visit the prisoners.

"I'd like to see the various people who were arrested in yesterday's drug raid, if that's possible," I told the officer at the desk of the county jail. He looked down at me from the raised desk (are those desks always built so high to make the visitor or the prisoner feel like a small child?), and he casually gazed at my black shirt, white collar, beard, and longish hair before looking back to the materials on his desk.

"Who are you?" he asked without looking at me again.

"My name is Tom Jackson. I'm co-director of the United Campus Ministry over on College Street. I've been asked by friends and family of some of the prisoners to visit them briefly, to see if they need anything."

"They go to your church?"

"Well, not exactly, because it's not a regular parish."

"Can't see the prisoners unless you're their preacher." He discarded the sentence along with a piece of paper from his desk.

"But we *are* ministers for the entire campus and town community," I responded, trying to gain his attention away from the plastic surface of his desk. "We don't have any membership regulations or . . ."

"Sorry, but those are the present rules," he said to his desk, interrupting my rather pathetic explanation of what U.C.M. was trying to do.

My suddenly empty mind and voice were spared immediate embarrassment by a call over the police radio, something about a drunk driver and an abandoned car. I took those few moments to think as fast as I could, to try to imagine *any* fact or credential or person who could help me in this petty power play. The frustration of being discounted as some uncertified preacher man was adding too much heat to the already stifling heat of the room. I could feel the sweat running down my chest, blotted here and there by the black shirt, providing visible evidence of checkmate. So it was time to change the rules of the little game, to take the offensive.

"Now listen, officer," I started with a mixture of respect and anger, "I'm an Episcopal priest assigned to this community by my bishop, with the clear support of the local Episcopal parish and the university administration. You may certainly call anyone at Good Shepherd parish or in Cutler Hall, and they'll vouch for my presence here."

"Sorry, but you'll have to come over here during regular visiting hours in a couple of days," he muttered to his pile of papers.

"Then I want to see the sheriff." My last card.

"Sheriff's busy."

"But I have to see him."

"Sheriff's *very* busy."

"Then I'll wait here until the sheriff's not very busy." I turned and sat down in one of the two metal folding chairs. The officer continued his desk work.

I sat for several long minutes, the sweat increasing with the rise in my anger. I stared at the floor, the walls, the county map, the partially opened sheriff's door. The only sounds came from the police radio, reporting the mundane facets of human foibles.

The outside door opened. A middle-aged woman guided in a little girl of about four years. The little girl's head was enveloped with bandages, and her hands were blotched with burns and gauze.

"Can I see my man for a minute or two?" the woman asked.

"No, ma'am, like I told you yesterday, you'll have to come over during regular visiting hours."

"But I just wanna show him what the hot water did to her."

"I'm sorry, but you'll have to wait a couple days. I'll tell him you were here." He was trying to be considerate, but he had his orders.

"Will you tell him that she's going to be all right?"

"I'll tell him that."

The woman left, the deputy disappeared into the sheriff's office, and I remained in the chair, my mind whirling with questions of power, prisoners, scalding water, red blotches, iron bars, and the absurdity of a five-thousand-dollar bail for smoking "grass."

A balding man in mufti accompanied the uniformed deputy

into the waiting room. I stood up as he announced, "I'm Sheriff Shields."

I quickly explained the situation again, trying not to acknowledge my previous difficulties with the deputy. The sheriff seemed preoccupied and anxious to get back to his room. He told me that I could talk briefly with the prisoners.

The male cell block was a large room; I could see a jungle of bunk beds, some of them occupied by shadows, with legs dangling over the sides. There was a small opening in the wall, just large enough for words, spoken or written, to pass through. A young man approached the hole on the other side.

"Hi," I started.

"Hi."

"My name's Tom Jackson—an Episcopal priest with the Campus Ministry. I've only got a few minutes, so I can't talk with everyone. Try to get any names and numbers of lawyers, parents, friends, or anyone who needs to be called. And a list of any toilet supplies you might need. Not just you guys who were busted yesterday, but the other prisoners as well. It's a hassle getting in here, so let's do it right and quickly."

"I will," he said quietly. As he turned away, I could see bodies jumping off bunk beds.

After a brief wait, I found a piece of paper coming through the hole, accompanied by the muffled words, "That's it, I guess."

"I'll try to do all of this and get back here soon. Without a lot of bullshit, can you tell me in confidence if you guys were clean or not?"

"I didn't have anything, and I think the others were clean, too. I just drove up to the house as the police arrived, and they busted me along with everyone else." He seemed unusually serene and almost content as he spoke. "There is one other thing, though."

"What's that?"

"Could you try to get a couple of books for me?"

"I'll try."

"I need a copy of the regular Bible and a copy of the *Aquarian Gospel.*"

"Are you serious?"

"Yes," he said gently. "They'll be good reading for jail time."

For my discussion with the seven or eight female prisoners, I was allowed to enter the cell, for the only other option was to yell through a steel door.

The female cell was unbelievable: no windows (with an inside temperature of at least 100 degrees), mattresses strewn about on the floor, and the heat-exaggerated smell of bodies, disinfectant, and toilet. With one or two exceptions, the women looked like "Betty Coed" rather than crime-hardened "addicts" as we so often think in our more lurid fantasies. I got the information as quickly as possible and escaped to the summer air.

As I left the jail, I discovered that Bob Hughes, the new, young assistant at the local Episcopal parish, had been hassled by the deputy too, and I felt a bit less paranoid. Outside the jail, I spoke with a sizable crowd of friends of the prisoners, although I had little to offer in the way of information or optimism. On the way to my car, I stopped by the police station and met Captain Cochran, and he seemed pointedly rude to me.

The hostility, confusion, and depression of this day was difficult to take. It was the thunderstorm which appears out of nowhere during an enjoyable picnic. It has changed my plans for a slow start here, and I know that already I have a reputation with the local police as a minister for "drug people." I don't get it—I've only been here one damned week!

August 24

The local paper, the Athens *Messenger*, covered the front of its Sunday edition with news and pictures of the drug bust. The pictures are those which only a newspaper photographer can take: den-of-iniquity shots, with everyone looking like Al Capone, and the police looking righteous and brave. Maybe the pictures paint an accurate picture, but my experiences yesterday do not seem to reflect it.

Another visit to the jail today, with little progress in any direction, although a couple of the prisoners were able to get the bond money. I spent some time this afternoon trying to get the local bondsman in gear, but it's a complicated process. He demands 10 percent in cash, and a local citizen must sign a promissory note, with property as security, for the balance. When the case is finally resolved, the bondsman gets a 10-percent fee. I guess it's a pretty good business, if you dig that sort of thing. If crime doesn't pay, at least defendants do.

August 30

It's been a week of jail visits, meetings with parents, and talks with the police. Several of the prisoners have been released on bond, but many others sit in jail because they don't have the cash. I've heard numerous definitions of freedom in my life, but this week I know that it refers clearly to the possession of money.

I've had a couple more discussions with Captain Cochran, and it becomes increasingly obvious that we are on two different wavelengths. The other day he bitterly asked why I never visited the jail to see the regular prisoners, why I only came to see the students. I tried to explain that I had only been in town for a couple of weeks, but he wasn't convinced. So I told him to appoint me as the chaplain of the jail, and then I would visit everyone as often as possible, without getting hassled by the deputies. He told me he would look into it. I'll bet.

Part of the problem in all of this is historical. It seems that last year, some of the local church members formed a "jail visitation" organization, and the group was allowed to talk with the prisoners at some length. After that went on for awhile, it became apparent that the visitors were discussing legal rights with the prisoners, while the police assumed that the visitors were only there to discuss religion. The program ended abruptly, with ill feeling on both sides. Of course, the losers in the situation were the prisoners—once again.

September 3

The hearings are being set by Judge Sheeter in the next couple of weeks, and I find that I have had time for little else. One of the girls has been practically catatonic since the initial arrest and, of course, she is the one without money for bail. She sits for hours without talking, has great difficulty in answering any questions, and seems totally withdrawn. A doctor has told me that her condition doesn't seem to be the result of heavy drugs; a friend of hers told me that "she has always been that way." And so, she finds herself locked in a windowless, suffocating room. Perhaps I would become catatonic, too.

A few students are starting to drift into town for the fall quarter, but the big rush won't come for about two more weeks. Considering the hostility already evident over this bust, I imagine that the student response is going to be wild, especially if the comments about student-police animosity are accurate.

Bill Black, the rector of the local Episcopal parish is very much "in" with the townspeople, the Chamber of Commerce, and the local power structure here in Athens. I understand that the local wheels have breakfast together every morning and discuss the daily gossip and political affairs. Bill called me today to tell me that his new assistant, Bob Hughes, and I had been discussed in some detail at the most recent breakfast. The gossip wasn't too damaging, although there was extended comment on the presence of beards on both clerical faces. I imagine that brands both of us as members of the International Commie Conspiracy to Destroy Morality and Fluoridate the Water. Anyway, Black is a good priest: he has decided to make the town his beat, and he's doing a good job of it; he is genuinely interested in his people.

September 15

I attended my first Campus Ministry Association meeting today. There are about fifteen men who represent every type and configuration of religious organization, although only eight or ten attend the meetings, I'm told. It was a low-key affair over a pleasant lunch, and the crowd was looking me over, asking the usual introductory questions and talking informally about the latest gossip. I guess we looked and sounded a lot like our local citizens' group that has breakfast together every morning at the cafeteria!

There is something a bit strange in meetings of local clergy groups. Maybe it's the same with realtors, insurance men, or funeral directors. There's an underlying feeling of mistrust or competition or overpoliteness. The members are very careful not to break the cardinal rule of ecumenicity: Thou shalt not make critical comments about another denomination's theology, customs, or liturgy. Consequently, very little gets done, and the main result is an agreement by the clergy to hold an ecumenical Thanksgiving service in the largest church in town.

That service is always perfectly mundane, and the clergy group spends the next six months talking about how nice it was, until it's time to plan the next one.

This general pattern is sometimes broken if the entire clergy group is composed of men from the same denomination. In that case, the formality might break into shoptalk and tongue-in-cheek comments about the latest scandal, the new bishop, or who's going to get which parish. Sometimes, the group will try to "relate on a gut level," which means that much of the hostility which has been brewing in the clergy-man's gut for the past six months will come rolling out in the form of tears, anger, or the shakes. I know of one such group in Jersey that got to the point of physical free-for-alls, which was fine for awhile, but then one guy was beating up everyone, and the group finally disbanded.

This campus clergy group might turn out to be okay, if we can get beyond the tuna-fish salad sometime. I'd rather get beaten up than do one of those inane Thanksgiving services.

September 17

In all of the mishmash of the past three weeks, of jails and courts and clergy and all the rest of it, I find myself sometimes incredulous about my role here, about what is expected of me by various people who are themselves acting out specific roles. Parents, bishops, faculty, students.

What am I supposed to be?

How often have I heard the same old line: "I'll bet you're very good with all those young people, you being so young and understanding those things they're always talking about."

That means that people think I am hip to what's going on.

But in the privacy of my own mind, I have to occasionally laugh uproariously at the very thought, for I am about as hip or as groovy as a glass of cold gravy. With a blush on my ego, I have to confess that I am really a GQ (Grooviness Quotient) flunky.

In fact, when it was last appraised, my GQ was listed at four points below that of Milton Berle. It's hard to sink that low, but for me it simply comes from a long history of being on the outside. And it's really kind of funny. To wit: at age eight, when marble-playing ability was the perfect GQ scale for me and my peer group, I lost 407 consecutive aggies and four steelies, in thumb-to-thumb competition. Instead of saying that I was "missing some of my marbles," people would point and say, "He hasn't got any of his marbles."

At the age of eleven, and standing five feet five inches, I discovered that my weight was listed on the doctor's chart at six feet three. I became a regular customer of the Husky Department at Robert Hall: "husky" is a pleasant euphemism so the salesclerk doesn't have to say, "Hmmm, your kid is short and fat." Fatness in itself was not always a negative GQ factor (Jowls Randolph, the bully down the block was considered groovy, but he could beat up everybody), but with me it simply meant that I weighed too much to play Little League football.

At age twelve, still rotund, I was sent to social-dancing school, in a desperate attempt at normality. When it was "boys' choice," all the groovy kids would streak across the floor to get first chance at the groovy girls. Every time I lumbered across, the only dancer left to choose was Peggy Gnome, who was also too heavy to play Little League football. Under similar circumstances, she ended up with me on the "girls' choice," so we danced a lot together; we weren't very good dancers, but no one got in our way.

Ages thirteen to eighteen are still too sensitive to be mentioned here; let me simply say that the increased grooviness potential of my fifty-pound weight loss was offset by a face covered with one inch of Clearasil.

My greatest chance for a high GO rating came when I

entered college in the early sixties. Back in those days, anyone who was groovy naturally belonged to a Greek house, so I quickly pledged. I was elected president of the pledge class. I was finally "in." But then they discovered that I didn't drink, that I wouldn't do errands for actives, and that I had fallen asleep during a lecture on the founding fathers of the fraternity. A month later, pledge-pinless, I was again out in the cold. But I was still ahead of Milton Berle.

When I discovered the wide acceptance of bleached-out jeans, I fantasized my splendor to the nearest jeans store. But I bought a too-baggy pair, and I underestimated the strength of bleach. As my wife accurately described the result, "Tom, they look like the bottom half of a clown's outfit."

At a time when motorcycles seem to represent everything that is groovy and heavy, I find myself making the wrong responses. When a "loaded chopper" goes sixty miles an hour down my street, with those "trumpet pipes" exhausting at about two hundred decibels, I don't get that sensual, groovy, masculine, competitive feeling of admiration: rather, I harbor demonic thoughts of sending a steel girder through the wheel spokes. Slowly, Milton Berle inches ahead of me.

As a remedy for my increasingly long hair and to fit in with some of the high-GQ crowd, I bought an official leather headband. The only time I wore it, I got the worst headache of my life.

With the *Playboy* adviser telling me that any combination of stripes-plaid-checks would look groovy on the Now scene, I proudly put on my new striped-plaid-checked tie-shirt-pants-coat. A girl, certified groovy by her jeans and work shirt, volunteered the opinion (uninvited) that my outfit was one of the ugliest combinations she had ever seen. I sulked home.

Groovy movies presented another chance to boost my GQ, but, of course, I blew it again. I began to understand what really was "in," and I went to all of the formula flicks. Some of them were sort of fun, and I began to feel like a member of the group. But my own lack of control finally destroyed this surefire GQ bonanza. Right there, in the middle of the ump-teenth groovy, formula flick, I *yawned*. I didn't mean to, but all of the R- and X-rated bare-ass guys and boob-swinging lovelies began to look alike to me. And one yawn followed another. I even began to have secret, unnatural fantasies of what all these people would look like with clothes on. I fell asleep. If that isn't bad enough, the next week I went to a non-groovy flick, and I got so involved in it that I cried. At that moment, I knew that my GQ potential was rapidly approach-ing zilch.

Well, the list of my low-GQ scores could go on indefinitely. If all of this isn't *exactly* true or if it has been exaggerated to maintain my own self-perspective, well, it matters not to those like myself who find themselves now-and-then at odds with what is considered "acceptable."

A very "in" girl told me recently: "What I'm really afraid of is that in a few years the Sears catalog will carry everything that we counterculture people are using as symbols now."

There are worse things to be afraid of, like trying to destroy each other because we have different symbols to express dif-fering ideas.

Or we can be afraid of the possibility of not occasionally laughing at our own overheated self-importance.

I pray that I can establish an important role here—and still laugh at my own absurdities.

September 18

The students are starting to pour in by the thousands, and the town seems to have a whole new feeling about it. They all look so different, so totally heterogeneous, so gloriously flip-pant. Longhairs, shorthairs, beautiful coeds, recent high schoolers, older grad students, strong ones, weak ones, jocks,

Greeks, and everything else you can categorize or imagine. It's great to see them outside my window, and I don't feel like such a stranger anymore.

Tom and Don (my co-workers) and I talked a bit about the Vietnam Moratorium which is supposed to take place in October and continue until the war ends. A couple of months ago, Tom agreed to have U.C.M. act as the local organizing representative, and we are excited about the possibilities of it. It will get U.C.M. involved in things at the very beginning of the year, and perhaps we can convince Nixon and his boys that this is an important issue to the people of this nation. It's worth another try.

I have heard from a few new acquaintances that the word is getting around campus very rapidly concerning the drug bust in August, and the hostility is obvious. The hearings in Judge Sheeter's court have left a lot of anger, and it is now apparent that there is simply no evidence in several cases. Stay cool, gang.

September 23

A bad scene this afternoon. A young coed named Barb was standing on the main street in town reading a mimeographed sheet which some guys were handing out, and she passed an extra one on to another student. At that moment, a couple of policemen busted her for distributing libelous materials. I think she was pretty harmless in the whole thing, but the mimeographed sheet was a bit heavy, including:

> Since last year, through the summer, and into the early fall, the thug racist Cochran-Sheeter power stucture has been busting people in Athens on trumped-up drug charges . . . drug busts are an excuse for the local pigs to come down on the youth culture. The purpose of this paper is to relate these local busts to nation-wide actions of the imperialist ruling class. And to

establish the beginnings of a self-defense network to deal with the pig-thug power structure.

The sheet continued with a listing of "rights during arrest," and a general warning to all students to "keep clean" of drugs. It was in many ways a childish effort, but I talked with many students this afternoon who showed great sympathy with it, not so much in terms of the hyperbole, but in the feeling of being attacked by the police for no apparent reason.

I visited Barb in jail tonight, and we made plans for the arrival, as soon as possible, of her parents. I realized in our discussion that she was anything but a "radical" student; but she was the one who had been apprehended.

As I left the jail, a voice in the shadows of the next building beckoned me, and I found myself talking sotto voce with a couple of male students. They didn't introduce themselves, but mentioned that they had had some responsibility in the production of the infamous mimeographed sheet, and they wanted to know how Barb was doing. I described the confines of her cell, and, as the anger rose within me, I suggested that they try to clear her of the charges. The conversation ended abruptly, and they were gone. It was like a bad movie.

September 26

About ten tonight I got a call about an emergency on a nearby street. I drove over as fast as I could. A crowd gathered in front of a shabby frame house. The whirling red lights from three police cars made it look like a scene from hell. A car from the local newspaper pulled up. The reporter jumped out and rushed up the steps. I made my way through the crowd. A friendly cop let me in. And what I saw was incredible.

A seventeen-year-old freshman had been given some acid, had freaked out, and had proceeded to literally tear the house apart. He was nude when the police arrived, and covered with the same feces he had frantically spread on the floors and walls. There was little to do at the house—it was a shambles—so I went to the university Health Center to visit him. We talked for only a few moments—he was still strung out, even after the relaxant drug—and I left.

I was angry by the time I got home, for I realized once again that this nation is one vast garden of misinformation about drugs. One person tells you that marijuana will destroy your life, and no facts are presented, no research is offered. Some other clown tells you that acid is the "ultimate trip to self," but ignores any facts which show the dangers. Why in the hell doesn't someone in this country do some homework on these issues?

September 29

Today's paper says that Dubcek and his followers are now officially silenced in Czechoslovakia. Russia is obscene, doing the same sort of power-politics crap that we've been pulling off in Vietnam for eight years.

It has always interested me that war protesters in the U.S. are incessantly assumed to be pro-Russia or pro-China. "If you don't like it here, why don't you go to Russia or China, you pinko bastard!" That's what we hear. Why? If I am upset with a policy or action taken by the U.S.—a policy or action which displays utter power hunger—why on earth should I want to go to live in a totalitarian regime which does the very same things? If the people of Russia and China want that sort of government—and I think they do—then they can have it, gladly. But I don't, and I'm very, very tired of eagle-encrusted American superpatriots telling me that criticism of my country is equal to support of some creeps who are also screwing people ten thousand miles away!

October 2

The Students for a Democratic Society (S.D.S.) sent a couple of representatives to Athens this week, and asked if they could hold a meeting in the basement of U.C.M., the room where the weekend coffeehouse operates. Tom and I talked it over and decided that a meeting would be permitted if it was open to the public. S.D.S. has become a frightening word to most of us, and we wanted to face it with some intelligence, rather than forcing the group off into some dark corner of the campus. I'm sure that we'll probably catch hell for letting them meet here.

Tom Niccolls was beautiful in the meeting. He patiently listened to all of the angry rhetoric and not-so-veiled threats. Then, right at the point of the hottest language, he quietly offered a nonviolent alternative. The young woman doing most of the talking was outraged by Tom's suggestion; she seemed capable of only screaming at him. But he timed his remarks perfectly, and they clearly offset the tempo of hate which she was trying to establish. It would have been easy for Tom to totally put her down, but he didn't; he simply tried to show that there were other alternatives.

I think everyone at the meeting was in agreement on the *issues* of Vietnam, distribution of goods, government controls, and all the rest, but the *means* were argued. The October 15 Moratorium is still a viable possibility for us, and Tom stated that we wanted to try that effort. Obviously, the woman saw us as a group of spineless, bankrupt liberals. Maybe she's right, but her approach sounded pretty crazy.

October 7

The *Messenger* carries the report of the death of Art Link-letter's daughter. It was a tragic death (if there is such a thing as a nontragic death), and perhaps Mr. Linkletter is right in claiming that the villain is hard drugs. It's obvious, though, that this is going to lead to more histrionics about drugs, instead of some government research and control. The government *could* stop the imports of heroin; it *could* start massive programs of investigation into the effects of various drugs; it *could* give the people facts, protection, and resources. I have to wonder why it doesn't.

October 9

We are pretty much in gear around U.C.M. now. The Draft Counseling Office, under the direction of David and Kate Reed, is working with scores of students. A group called "Appalachian Student Volunteers" is trying to get information and organization into the Appalachian communities around here, but it's often a frustrating job. So many of the people have been poor for generations, and they seem to accept that as their fate.

Student Tutors for Educational Progress (S.T.E.P.) is working closely with U.C.M., and we attempt to give them as much support as possible. These hundreds of volunteer tutors go into the area schools several times each week to supplement the instruction in the basic reading and writing skills.

The third floor of the house offers a home for the Ohio Program in International Living, an organization which allows seven or eight students from various nations to live together each year. It's not a terribly structured program, and the students can learn from each other in a reasonably "normal" atmosphere.

The basement houses the "Cellar Door," a coffeehouse which operates mainly on the weekends, and provides space for university classes and meeting during the week.

Our "open door" policy here is not appreciated by everyone, for we often hear that we should exclude "left-wingers" or "right-wingers" or "R.O.T.C. types" or others. Consequently, we let everyone in, and our new policy statement says that any meetings can be held here if they are open to the public and if violent acts are not planned in those meetings. Naturally, many university administrators and townspeople are a bit upset, but it seems to be the only way we can go if we are to take the Christian label seriously.

October 11

The Weathermen are rampaging in Chicago, and the scene is made even more surrealistic by the trial of the Chicago Seven. I have met and talked with a few of the people who went to Chicago for this "event," and I know that at least two of them are already under arrest. I know the utter frustration which compels them to act (as I sit smug and comfortable in my carpeted office), and yet I regret the suicidal aspect of their behavior. I cannot tell them not to go; I know that our actions of murder and devastation in Southeast Asia are monstrous compared to their window breaking in the Loop. They will be called insane and childish for these acts, but who has led them to this point? We can search for all of the scapegoats we want, but the answer is written on our own 500-pound bombs, as they glide toward thatched roofs.

October 12

A memorable day, for better or worse.

This past week I agreed to participate in a "Community Dialogue" held in Memorial Auditorium today. The thing had been billed as an opportunity for students to communicate with Judge Franklin Sheeter, police Capt. Charles Cochran, a couple of local lawyers, myself—and Edgar Whan, a magnificent, sensitive English prof as moderator.

The occasion was prompted by the rapidly growing hostility of many students toward the police and municipal court. In addition, Pres. Claude Sowle had announced on September 24 that he was attempting to initiate a program of drug control, in which first offenders might be dealt with on the basis of university discipline, rather than court action. The response from the local government officials has not seemed overwhelmingly enthusiastic.

Several hundred people packed the auditorium this afternoon, and I was placed at a table with Sheeter and Cochran on the stage, while other panelists sat nearby at similar tables. Edgar Whan initiated the onstage discussion, and then the discussion was opened to questions from the floor. The atmosphere was highly hostile in all directions, and the student response was similar to a Saturday-afternoon matinee: cheers for the "good guys" and boos for the "bad guys."

After charges and countercharges had been hurled in reference to the August drug bust, someone asked each of us at my table what we would do if we caught our sons smoking marijuana. Hoo boy.

Judge Sheeter showed no hesitation: "I would kick him out of the house." It was just the response that the students expected, and it took Whan a few minutes to quiet the place down.

Captain Cochran was visibly shaken by the question, and I think that he tried to be sensitive in his response. He briefly described his relationship with his son, which was corny but nice, and ended with: "I can't answer that now, though it would hurt me terribly to know that he had committed that crime." Again, the audience was not in a mood to accept Cochran's sudden gentleness, and there was another noisy response.

When it was finally my turn to respond, I mentioned that Judy and I had tried marijuana once a couple of years ago, and that we had each experienced a "bum trip" on the strong stuff we had. I added that I knew of numerous people who had had an enjoyable experience with it, but that I was concerned that people were "turning off" from reality with it, just at the time when I want people "turned on" to our chaotic world. The response to my statement was more surprise than anything else, and the meeting ended within the hour.

I think the whole fiasco was a mistake. It didn't increase understanding or dialogue; rather, it confirmed all of our mutual prejudices. I got angry with the audience at a couple of points, for whenever Cochran would make a grammatical error, there would be audible laughter. That's crap as far as I'm concerned.

Whoever thought this one up had better get back to the drawing board.

October 13

The coverage of the "Community Dialogue" in the *Messenger* and the university *Post* was rather complete, although my statement on my experience with marijuana was a bit too prominent, and I will probably be seen as the "addicted priest" before long. *No one* is going to believe that we only tried it once, and once is too often for most readers anyway. Oh well.

Nixon announced today that the planned Moratorium activities will only help the North Vietnamese.

October 14

The staff met today, and we made our final preparations for the Moratorium tomorrow. We are becoming very close, and I need that.

Spiro and Senator Scott both commented today that the planned Moratorium activities are "communist-oriented and supported." I want to yawn and ignore them . . . but Agnew forces my attention, and I resent that.

One hundred and seventy-four profs here have signed a statement supporting the Moratorium, and 125 of them are planning to cancel classes.

October 15

The day has arrived! The expectation, the nervousness, the hope of it all were uniquely satisfied. For the first time in months, I felt as if I were actually a part of my country, however confused and fallible it might be.

The sights and sounds and feelings were delicious to me, even when we encountered a few negative reactions on the street. The people involved—students, faculty, townspeople, old, young, black, white, yellow—were *gentle* in this first massive protest (and, God, I hope it doesn't end here).

Workshops on all aspects of the war were well attended.

The bright sun, the autumn air and leaves, the closeness of people, the lushness of green grass, all of it unforgettable.

About three thousand people walked in a Silent March

through town, starting and ending on the College Green. It was an incredible sight—hundreds and hundreds of people winding their way through city streets, wearing black armbands, answering not a word when a bystander now and then would yell "Commies!" or "Traitors!" or "Troublemakers!"

As the March ended, a black student played taps, and several other students began reading the list of thousands of names of young Americans who had died in this obscene war, and each name was followed by the deep thump of a bass-drum beat. It was an eerie scene, and it went on for hours as each of the dead was momentarily resurrected in our corporate mind and gut.

It was certainly a day of exhilaration in community and sorrow in memory, but, more than anything else, it was the day of Tom Niccolls' speech. A few excerpts of his truth:

I want to talk about fear, for fear is at the heart of this war—fear of communism, fear of losing face by admitting a mistake, fear of losing profits, fear of seeing the truth about America.

A generation ago, a president spoke of freedom from fear, and we hope that someday it will come. But so long as many fears are with us, it is time to ask, what shall we be afraid of? It is time to ask: what fears make for life, and what fears make for death? The question is: what fears shall we choose to honor? . . . There is fear here. There is fear of legislators and judges who threaten university dissenters with repressive laws and cut budgets. There is fear in the student who does not challenge this business-as-usual attitude of his classes, while the longest war in American history continues. There is fear in the businessman and fear in the clergyman, that if they speak out, they will certainly lose their customers and congregations.

Those are the fears that press upon us, and to some degree, none of us escape . . .

But we can choose other fears. . . . We are afraid that our humanity will cease to be. . . . We are afraid for the soul of America; we are afraid for our humanity, if we let this war continue. . . . We are disturbed that America seems no longer able to distinguish truth from falsehood—propaganda from fact—

slogan from reality. The illusions, the myths, the falsehoods, and the lies that support the carnage and destruction in Vietnam have been repeated so often they begin to sound like truth . . .

Not only that, but we are even more afraid for our hearts. . . . We are deeply troubled that men will lose their humanity so much that they will no longer shudder when a military leader like Patton says, "I like to see those arms and legs fly." We are afraid that we will become dehumanized by the logic of the major at Be Tre last year, who said, "It became necessary to destroy the town in order to save it." We are terrified at seeing ourselves in the chaplain who admires his soldiers gathering to pray and then says, "And not only that, they are bloody good killers, too."

And we march because we are afraid for our wills, our will to resist this gross distortion of our national priorities. We dissent because we are afraid of turning into a nation of Eichmanns, obediently falling into line in the name of national unity and national pride . . .

It comes down to something like this: do we have the will to reorder our values—do we have the courage to turn around? The administration wants *five billion* dollars this year for ammunition to shoot the enemy, and *three billion* for school children in America. If you divide the number of North Vietnamese and NLF soldiers and the number of American school children into those respective figures, it comes out this way: our government wants to spend $200,000 to shoot an enemy soldier, and $44 to educate an American child!

But we can stop. We can halt business-as-usual before the whole business destroys our minds and our hearts and our wills. . . . We have the deepest sympathy for those who back the war because they have sons and fathers and lovers and husbands in Vietnam. But even they must understand that even if *all* 500,000 Americans died in Vietnam, that would not make the cause one whit more sacred or right. This is hard to understand when we think of the thousands who have died . . .

How much better to honor the dead by laboring for peace, by lobbying for peace, by constantly writing letters for peace, by talking for peace. If we make no effort to break the threat that hangs over the world from modern man's weaponry, if we make no effort to force our leaders to relieve the long-suffering of the people in Vietnam, then we will be judged guilty of the crimes and the abominations that will continue to emerge from this war.

What are we afraid of? That is truly the question.
When we are afraid that our humanity shall cease to be, then perhaps we shall begin to live!

The crowd was silent for a few seconds, and then it burst into applause and cheers and yells and hope. The clapping was thunderous and seemingly endless, and Tom—in his humility not expecting such a response—found it difficult to accept the outpouring of that throng of people. I knew what he was feeling, but I wanted him to know the depths of appreciation which were being offered to him. I wonder if he knew.

I think that I shall sleep well tonight, if I can forget the beating of the bass drum for awhile.

October 21

Don and I tried to tell Tom how proud we were of him at the Moratorium and how upset we were that he seemed unable to accept the tremendous outpouring of applause and admiration after his magnificent speech. The conversation was increasingly producing heavy thoughts and emotions, when—suddenly— a small, rubber monkey fell out of Tom's breast pocket, bounced off his leg, and rolled to a stop in the middle of the office floor. All of us momentarily looked at the thing, trying to figure where in the hell it came from—and we broke into convulsive laughter that simply wouldn't stop. We laughed until the tears flowed—we gasped for air—we laughed more until our stomachs and sides would not permit any more. Tom tried to explain amidst the sighs and gasps that the monkey must have been put in his pocket by his young daughter . . .

And then there was silence.

Each of us knew that we had just shared a sacred event, that a crazy rubber monkey, placed in innocence by a child, had been our bread and wine, our sacrament. In the quietness that followed, we tried to relate to each other the bonds of our

Calvinistic upbringing—the ambiguous message of the Church that we should somehow feel guilt over personal accomplishments, just as the cliché-ridden home-run hitter must publicly emphasize the "team effort," rather than his own effort—"Oh, I was just lucky, I guess."

God tells us to love ourselves—to accept ourselves for what we are and what we can be—but we want so much to deny it, to say that we are ultimately unacceptable. How often I see this in my counseling, and yet I do little to heal myself of its unrealistic demands on my person.

In the tears of confession and in the silence of mutual absolution, the three of us knew that we were now a community—and the "day of the rubber monkey" shall never be forgotten.

October 26

I discovered again today the real meaning of worship and celebration.

I had been asked by a young couple—who are not "churched"—to baptize their infant son. We decided to do the thing at Dow Lake, which is a few miles from Athens, and they invited about forty of their friends. When we arrived at the site, a park ranger suddenly appeared, and told us that we couldn't perform a baptism in the lake because it was state property. I understood his position, and yet I didn't want to ruin the occasion—so we compromised: I would take water *out* of the lake, and do the baptism on the shoreline. Everyone was satisfied.

Amidst the stares of curious onlookers, we proceeded with the rites, emphasizing the child's membership in the Family of Man, as well as the Kingdom of God (that may mean the same thing!). At the end of the formally spoken words, I decided instantly that I wanted the people there to *experience* this new human being, this new brother in life, and so I had the baby passed around the congregation, which was sitting on the side of a hill. From hand to hand, young Ian was felt, smelled, fondled, kissed, and simply held. There was much laughter, a few tears, and a corporate understanding that a baptism is not a passive event, but a "welcome to life" party to be shared by all.

October 27

I participated in another panel discussion last night, this one on "Student Rights." There were a few university administrators in attendance, plus a large, brilliant, articulate black woman named Lillian Ramos, who is here this year as a prof in the new Black Studies Institute. Her comments were magnificent. As a woman, a lawyer, a world traveler, and sensitive human being, she could listen and *then* speak. She knew the whole idea of "student as nigger," and she offered *real* ideas for a change.

Lillian and I had a cup of coffee afterwards. She was not uptight about my whiteness, but allowed me to share a bit of her life. I'm glad she's here.

October 29

A female client came to see me, a woman in her late thirties or early forties. She wanted to know how to increase the communication with her husband of some twenty-odd years. I don't know. Caress him, question him, kick him, startle him, I don't know. Will he go to a counselor with her? No, probably not. Will he talk with her? He hasn't lately. Does *he* think that there's a problem? No. How often is there some sort of sexual expression? Intercourse on rare occasions, caresses hardly at all. What else bothers her? It's a small town, a "company town," and she feels out of place most of the time. And bored. And resentful. Tell me more . . .

Prescription: try to get him to talk, to see you again as his wife, his bedmate, his friend. Just try to get his attention for awhile and tell him how you feel, but do it gently.

I really don't know.

October 30

If you ever want to draw a crowd, have a panel discussion on *sex!* We packed 'em into the South Green cafeteria tonight, and I faced the assembled masses with a Health Center doctor, a counselor, and a moderator. To lessen the underlying embarrassment, we took *written* questions from the floor, and they were incredible!

Can I get syph from a toilet seat? You need direct contact with an infected person.

Does masturbation really lead to insanity? Only if you're crazy.

What is onanism? A rather bleak attempt by ancient churchmen to interpret a Bible passage so that people would think that God destroys anyone who masturbates.

What should I do if I think that a guy on our dormitory floor is a homosexual? Treat him as a human being.

What is all of this stuff about cancer in women who take the pill? A very low incidence, but you should always have a complete physical before getting the pill; it appears that pregnancy causes more maternal deaths than does the pill.

There were many more questions dealing with everything from abortion to "zits" (will sex really clear up my blemishes?), and I was left with the impression that we are acting criminally by not offering more sex education to these young people in high school. All of the old myths abound, and it's overwhelming.

I gave a short rap on the difference between "sex" and "sexuality," the latter being an expression of the whole person, rather than just the limited act of intercourse. I think it bored them.

November 2

The campus ministry at the University of Michigan has gotten a lot of coverage in the media, so Jude and I took some students for a visit to Ann Arbor this weekend. We had a good time, although I came to see that we cannot import another ministry to our campus. What they are doing there is good for them; we've got to do our own thing.

The visit included a quick trip to Detroit to see my old parish again. It was depressing. The ghetto has clearly gotten worse, and I could fathom almost no changes in the area since I left eighteen months ago. Worse poverty, more winos, less action —in essence, a dying city.

During the week of the Detroit riots in '67, I asked a black guy why all of the buildings were being destroyed. Obviously angered by my naïveté, he said, "Well, brother, when you white folks get pissed off at life, you borrow some cash and head for Miami Beach. As you look at these burning buildings, you are looking at our trip to Miami Beach. Dig?"

"Yeah."

"And now you're going to ask about our big cars, right?"

I protested, to no avail.

"Well, brother, my car is my mobile living room. It gets me the hell out of this hole, and whitey can't limit me too much on where I want to go. The cops out in Grosse Pointe might follow me awhile to make sure I'm not going to burglarize one of them fancy houses, but they can't push me off the street, not while I'm driving that car. See, Father, you learn something new every fuckin' day, right?"

November 5

Tom and I have been doing a "midnight Mass" sort of thing in the coffeehouse on Saturday nights, with just the people who come in off the street. The crowds have been numbering about fifty or sixty, and several of the bread-and-wine services have been emotionally satisfying for all of us, regardless of our Church membership or lack of same. It's starting to get heavy, though, for the mixture of viewpoint in the "congregation" is so great that many theological questions are literally getting in the way of our celebration together. I hate to see this thing happen, for the memories of parish squabbles are too vivid. I think we'll cancel the services for a couple of weeks and try to figure things out.

November 10

The Athens Peace Committee (the name finally agreed on for the antiwar group here) met tonight, and finalized plans for the Moratorium in Washington, D.C., this week. Everyone is excited about the possibilities, and hundreds of people are planning to go from here, by car, by bus, and by thumb. There were the usual discussions about the need for nonviolence, and I think we can accomplish that.

A freshman came to me this week for help; he wants to go to D.C., but his father, thinking that the whole affair is commie oriented, refuses to grant permission. I wrote a long letter to the father, suggesting that the young man be allowed to make a personal decision on this one; if he has been given understanding in his upbringing, then he will certainly have the intelligence to judge the event for whatever it is.

The freshman has been given permission to go, and I feel good about it.

November 16

We are back from Washington and from the exhilaration, frustration, ecstasy, depression, joy, success, and failure of the Moratorium.

I had lived in Greater Washington for three years, and the anticipation of returning seemed to grow steadily as our car reached too-high speeds on the way. Perhaps it was the irony of fear. I must get closer to the monster to see if it really breathes fire.

These feelings were compounded by sight and sound, of seeing the Northern Maryland suburbs in the darkness of Thursday night, while listening to the innuendos of Agnew's speech on the radio. The anger I felt was not so much a product of the little man's words (they were so typical and so obvious, and I knew that there would be many more in the months to come), but rather the thoughts they engendered of the deputy attorney general suggesting that all the militants be put in concentration camps, with the Veterans' Day speeches of treason and the Moratorium, of the knowledge of thousands of army troops waiting in those same Maryland suburbs. The little man would not let the fear alone.

Thursday night, Friday morning, Friday night, Saturday morning—all melted into one continuous hassle of keeping the headquarters of the church in order, of changing plans, of housing a couple of hundred people instead of twenty, of discovering that the church was very uptight about our presence, of finding the main phone locked within an office for which we could not have a key, of lost people and twisted-ankle people, of a constant search for toilet paper and more food, and the same pervading fear that "something is going to happen."

But it was a hassle to celebrate, a good hassle, a hassle which makes you want to stay awake for no rational reason, a hassle which says, "Okay, I'll live through the fear if I can live through it with these people!"

The March against Death can, for me, be summed up in the moment when that father paused in front of the White House and screamed out the name of his dead son, with no speech attached to the words, just the name; he couldn't see the White House because of the light shining in his face, but those same lights reflected the tears and the anger and incredible loss which showed on his face.

Yes, I yelled out "Kenneth Krist" as I walked by, but Kenneth was an unknown brother to me, not my son. God, I don't want to ever know that feeling which those lights showed on that face . . .

I can't offer too much in terms of the march which took place on Saturday, only a few sights and sounds. The kid with the Viet Cong flag in one hand and a Kodak Instamatic in the other; the feeling of walking with a hundred thousand people on Pennsylvania Avenue, and looking to the left to see another two hundred thousand walking in a parallel direction on the Mall; of seeing the fisted-glove-hand of the cop directing us along, and then seeing the hand open with a peace button pinned to the leather palm; Jerry Rubin suggesting that we were only "making peace respectable" (*but that's what I want to do, Jerry*), of wondering what was going on in Athens as I walked toward the Monument . . .

There's really no reason to go on with this. Dickens was "right on" with the bit about the best of times and the worst of times; it was, and is, just that. It was staggeringly beautiful and ultimately frustrating, but what else is new!

God, I hope that something is new . . . something.

November 18

I think things are going to get hot around here after today's events.

For the last couple of months, a young man named John Kirkendall has spent hundreds of hours in U.C.M., talking with people generally, and seeking counsel from Tom and me. John has been in the Naval Reserve, and, beginning in July, he quit going to the weekly sessions in Parkersburg. He is a very troubled young man: quiet, gentle, trying to figure out his thoughts and feelings about himself, his participation in the armed services, and his theology. If anything is obvious, it's that John is sincere in his questions and beliefs.

I have talked with John on numerous occasions, and I know that he has attempted to go through the proper channels to resign from the service, all to no avail. He recently had a Naval hearing on this matter, and the report of it was sent to him, showing that he is being nominated for immediate active duty as a "punishment" for his behavior. On the back of his orders was written the following report from his commanding officer, and I reproduce it exactly as written:

> It is the Command's position that this individual is insincere in his belief's and he has been dupped by leftist-passifist associates. If this individual is permitted to break his enlistment contract through this means, it is very likely to open the lid to Pandora's Box. It is therefore contended that this nomination to immediate active duty is the appropriate course of action to take.

I discussed the possibility of applying for a conscientious-objector discharge with John, but he is adamant in refusing to go that route; such an alternative, he says, is a cop-out, for it uses the very system he opposes. He adds that he is ready to go to jail if the navy refuses to release a human being who has decided that military activity is immoral. I suppose that if John has been "duped" by anything, it is the Bible.

So, this afternoon, John officially asked for "sanctuary" at U.C.M. until he is arrested. He says that U.C.M. is his church, and he is turning to this community for support. As Tom, Don, and I did not have a chance to speak with our Board, we did the only thing possible within the Christian spirit as we understand it: we granted him sanctuary.

There was a picture in the paper today of a soldier named William Calley, who is being investigated at Fort Benning for the murder of 109 civilian Vietnamese at a place called My Lai.

Who is really being duped?

November 19

Tom Niccolls and I released a statement to the newspapers, explaining as best we could why we are giving sanctuary to John.

At tonight's monthly Board meeting, our statement was given a vote of confidence—after lengthy discussion—with only two negative votes: one because "we shouldn't take the law into our own hands," and the other because "a man should not break a contract, regardless of his change in feelings." With that last comment, I thought immediately of the guys who were *contracted* to build the extermination ovens in Germany, but I kept my mouth shut.

I am thankful for the support we got.

November 20

This afternoon we celebrated a bread-and-wine service for John, and several people participated; I noticed that people who had never before taken the bread or the wine did so to-day, and that seemed important to them. At the end of the service, I left the remaining elements out on the table in the main lounge, so that others might come in later to partake of the symbol of this community. I guess we could call it, in High Church fashion, the *un*reserved sacrament!

November 22

As I think about the consistent support I've been receiving from the Board here, I am increasingly able to laugh at some of the trivialities which happened in Jersey and Detroit and seminary and so forth. I guess that I wasn't able to laugh at the original situations, though.

About two weeks before I was asked to leave the Jersey parish a warden—or "head layman" of the parish—came to my office for a "talk." A wealthy man in his early seventies, he said that he wanted to discuss something that had been bother-ing him for some time.

"What is it?" I inquired rather nervously.

"It's the increase of your hair," he said directly and force-fully.

"The increase of my hair?"

"Yes. You arrived here last summer clean-shaven and with a nice haircut. It looked very clean-cut. Then I noticed that you had grown a moustache."

"Yes."

"Then, awhile later, I noticed that you had grown a beard."

"Yes, sort of a goatee, because I don't have a very full beard on the side."

"Yes, well then I began to notice that your hair was getting longer and starting to hang over your collar."

"Yes?"

"Well, I want to know what your plans are in the future."

"About my hair?"

"Yes, about your hair."

"I suppose," I started with genteel anger, "that there isn't too much more to worry about because I seem to have run out of places to grow hair. But I'll probably keep what I have now, at least until I get tired of it, and then I'll probably cut it all off."

"I see," he concluded, and left abruptly.

Once he told me that he and his wife had fervent hopes that my wife would grow into a great clergy wife or, as he put it, an "Amazon of Faith." But he didn't know who my wife was after four months of our presence in the parish.

Then there was the woman in Detroit who said that I stuck out my tongue at her whenever I served her Communion. I told her that wasn't true as far as I knew, and she yelled, "How dare you call yourself a priest!" The logic escaped me.

And there was the professor in seminary who was afraid that our newspaper-sponsored dialogue on homosexuality would turn many of the students into "homos." I don't think it did.

Have I been on Candid Camera for the past five years?

November 30

Two days ago, while all of us on the staff were away for Thanksgiving vacation, Captain Cochran went to U.C.M. and arrested John Kirkendall—then to Logan, where the naval officers took him for incarceration in the brig in Columbus.

Local law officers receive rewards for "apprehending" military personnel.

Happy Thanksgiving, John.

December 9

This afternoon I talked with a sensitive young faculty member who is in a family crisis. He has had a pretty good relationship with his wife, but the vigoro has just hit the fan. Many months ago, in another city, he had a brief affair with another woman, and she recently wrote him a letter—which his wife found and read today.

I find marriage counseling to be the toughest counseling I do. It assumes, hopefully, a continuing relationship between two people. Therefore, how do you deal with the hurt, the disappointment, the anger, the *history* of it all? One can ask and hope for forgiveness, and yet the proximity of the two people allows for so many chances to retaliate, sulk, or openly suffer.

This one's going to take a lot of work.

December 13

We held a festive surprise party for Jude's twenty-seventh birthday last night, and the noise of dozens of people enjoying good wine and food and love echoed throughout the evening.

We have a big, old house which is a superb place for entertaining, and we enjoy that so much. After weeks of painting and wallpapering and spending money, we are progressing toward the kind of warmth we want in the house. I am very jealous of my home: I need it desperately after the days and nights of work here; it becomes an oasis for my weary psyche.

Jude is so totally Jude. We set aside "our time" each evening at about eleven, when we are undisturbed by the kids, the job, the world. We can talk about our crazy existence, or make love, or simply lie in each other's arms—or all of those things. It is a beloved ritual for me, one which constantly brings me back to her, the person who is ultimately concerned with my life. It is such an urgent thing for me. And I am often disturbed to discover that many of my married clients do not set aside such a personal time in their lives.

Rabbi Joe Polak describes the sabbath as a holy time for contemplation, when the meaning of life can be brought into sharp focus. That is my time with Judy—my daily sabbath— and I protect it as much as I celebrate it.

December 17

I just got back from three days at Procter Farm—the diocesan conference center—where we held a conference for the Board of Managers and staff. It was absolutely magnificent.

The Board decided to go along with the staff plans to repaint and renovate much of the U.C.M. building. Although it is a commitment of a few thousand dollars to "brick and mortar," it seems acceptable as long as the *whole* building is being used *all* week. That is my major hang-up with property programs in parishes: hundreds of thousands of dollars are spent, and then the building is used once or twice a week.

I am reminded of the parish we attended in D.C. during seminary days. Actually, it was a mission started by an unusually talented priest named Al Shands. We met for worship in a famous seafood restaurant on Sunday mornings—before the eating crowd arrived—and the city authorities decided that we must drape a white sheet over the restaurant bar during our liturgy! The local bishop allowed us to adapt the regular Morning Prayer and Eucharist services to the setting, and it was superb. A couple of years later, the congregation had to move into a new building which the diocese had built for us, although it had been planned so that everything in the building was movable, and could be used by different groups throughout the week.

A building, though, is a problem and it can become the reason for being. It's dangerous. Perhaps I'm too oriented to the security of it all.

Anyway, I'm delighted with the events of the past two days.

December 18

I became a film star today, although it was unintentional . . . at least on my part.

I officiated at a wedding for a young Chinese couple in the campus chapel, and all of their Chinese friends from the state of Ohio showed up. No sooner had I opened my mouth to start the wedding, than it seemed that every person in the chapel jumped up and started taking pictures. To my right was a 16-mm. movie camera whirring off memories to be sent back to Hong Kong for mom and dad; to my left were several 35-mm. cameras clicking for every motion, every word, every facial expression—with one fellow straddling the altar rail for a better angle! It was out of control, and I knew it. The couple standing in front of me was undaunted by the bedlam, and I decided to go along with it, doing sort of a ventriloquist routine of saying the words while trying to smile into the cameras. The bride faltered in her English about halfway through the service, so she took to nodding, and once, for good measure, the groom answered for her.

I got them married, though, and they exited amidst the continued clicking—and I'm sure that I will be famous in Hong Kong before long.

December 25

Our first Christmas in Athens is beautiful. And, of course, we have overbought for the kids and each other, a typical American tradition.

Jennifer, at three our oldest, is just starting to comprehend all that is going on around her. We adopted her in Virginia just before seminary graduation, and she looks very much like both of us. She is probably being spoiled by the attention she receives from the many students who come to the house, but I approve of the extended family idea, especially if it brings love.

Peter is eleven months old now and appears more sure of himself. His Jewish mother and his black father must have been attractive people, for he is becoming a beautiful child. He has been with us now for seven months, and I think he may decide to stay.

In all, it is a time when we can each be a child again, to relive the memories of other Christmases with other beloved people, even as we remember the agony of this day in Southeast Asia.

We must celebrate when we can.

II

Well, I don't know what will happen now. We've got some difficult days ahead, but it really doesn't matter with me now because I've been to the mountaintop. And I don't mind. Like anybody, I would like to live a long life. Longevity has its place. But I'm not concerned about that now, I just want to do God's will. And He has allowed me to go up to the mountain. And I've looked over, and I've seen the Promised Land. I may not get there with you, but I want you to know tonight that we as a people will get to the Promised Land. So I'm happy tonight. I'm not worried about anything. I'm not fearing man. Mine eyes have seen the glory of the coming of the Lord.

—Martin Luther King, Jr.

January 14, 1970

With the coincidence of Martin Luther King's birthday and the observance of the Moratorium tomorrow, the Athens Peace Committee has erected—with permission—a cardboard "village" on the College Green to represent Resurrection City and My Lai. The spirits of the group members seem rather low at this point, for the enthusiasm for the Moratorium has waned. Maybe this will pick them up a bit.

I let it be known that I am celebrating a few Requiem Masses tomorrow in memory of King, and I have been hassled all afternoon about it. One administrator sounded as though we were going to bring in the Second Coming prematurely.

"There are a thousand ways of saying no to life, and one way of saying yes."

I wonder if the author of that famous quote would accept a new ending to it: ". . . and if you attempt to say yes to life, a thousand people will try to convince you that a no is better judgment."

As I write these words on this late Wednesday evening, I now have serious questions about my own ability to "do my own thing," and that is difficult to admit. In the past forty-eight hours, I have been hassled by all quarters.

I have been told by the university not to get near Cutler Hall with a Requiem Mass.

One "official" has suggested that it would be sacrilegious to do a Requiem near Cutler or in the Frontier Room or anyplace outside of a church (as a campus minister, I do not *have* a church, but I do *experience* a church).

Some students suggested that since King was black, I should not claim him as one of my own because I am white.

An "official" and some students decided that I should not celebrate an Episcopal liturgy around campus, for I would be forcing people to accept my beliefs (I was not asked if I was actually using such a liturgy).

Other students told me I would be derided by everyone if I tried a Requiem in the Frontier Room at noon or any other time.

And then there were more implications about going near Cutler Hall . . .

Okay, I've gotten the message. Yes, I have understood the implications. I am *not* a hero. I do not want to be hated or derided or embarrassed or even ignored. If I am an affront to people, I apologize; if my beliefs are disgusting to others, I do not wish to force them. But, as corny as it may sound, I do believe that Martin was my brother, both in humanity and our ministry, and I shrink before his example; I do protest this carnage in Vietnam, as he was called to do; I do celebrate those people who have gotten involved in life, and I protest their countless murders. I know that I do not have the courage of those people, but the *least* I can do is celebrate their lives tomorrow with the simple acts of my own vocation.

I wonder if it's all worth the hassle.

January 15

The two masses on the College Green were sparsely attended (although television cameras whirred), but the great feeling came in the Frontier Room of the student center, the place where most of the so-called hippies hang.

At noon, nervous as hell, Tom Niccolls and I walked in. About 150 people filled the room. The jukebox blared. We sat at a table for a few minutes, and then, collecting my courage, I stood up and yelled at the top of my voice: "Today is the anniversary of the birth of Martin Luther King, Jr., and I would like you to join me in a bread-and-wine celebration of his life among us . . ."

I waited for a moment as the noise continued—and then someone walked over to the jukebox and yanked the cord from the outlet. There was silence. Slowly, all the people in that room, most of whom hadn't seen the inside of a church in years (and cared less), moved slowly toward our end of the room. We proceeded to celebrate without embarrassment or silver chalices—we used the bond of corporate concern and the ceramic cup I had been given for the baptism at the lake.

God, it was a magnificent experience.

I hope that we never forget King. It is now "in" to deride him, to say that he had lost hold of the leadership in the movement.

But who brought the movement out of its infancy?

Who was prisoner 7089 in the Montgomery jail?

Who marched in endless paths of righteous protest?

Who brought the issue of pervasive poverty to our middle-class conscience?

Who dared tie the despicable war to the movement?

Who had his throat shot out while attempting to shout the basic dignity: "I am a man!"?

Who did all of that? King.

If the spirit of the King is dead, so are we.

January 18

Amidst a glorious community of fellowship, I was "officially installed" as co-director of U.C.M. today, with song, embarrassing words, and good food. Tom Niccolls presented a multimedia program and university Vice-President Dorf suggested publicly that I should not be distressed by the administrative hassles which were so apparent on King's birthday. I was overwhelmed by the generosity of so many.

January 23

I don't really know what to do about Tom Niccolls. He is in the process of finishing his thesis, will probably get his Ph.D. this summer, and will then be ready and qualified to teach. I know that I *should* push him hard to get it done, to find a teaching job somewhere, to explore some new horizons.

But I'm selfish.

I don't want him to leave. It is too good a thing, this working relationship we have. We know how to share our perceptions and our responsibilities and our lives.

I know that he dreams to teach.

I also know that there is really—finally—no choice involved. He will leave, he will teach, and he will be superb at it.

I wonder if there's a way to get him a job here in Athens?

January 25

I'm brooding about John Kirkendall. In December, he was taken from the brig in Columbus to the brig at the naval station in Philadelphia. A minister in Philly was able to get John a really sharp attorney, and it looked as though he might be able to present a strong case to the navy. Then, a couple of weeks ago, he suddenly walked off the naval base and fled to Canada.

He called me long-distance from Toronto; he sounded sad, lonely, confused. He felt that he could not go through with the whole thing, that he would have to "sell out" in the process.

Here I sit, sulking in disappointment because John didn't go through with the plan as I understood and accepted it. A guy who has gone through a catharsis in the past six months is frantically trying to find his life in Canada, overwhelmed by the events which led him there—and I sit here judging him!

Who the hell am I anyway?

How often have I had the courage to do an absolute about-face in my life when I realized that my actions might be immoral? John did. And now he desperately needs support.

Sometimes, Jackson, you stink.

January 29

This afternoon, Lillian Ramos, the strong, demanding, gentle black history prof, died of an apparent heart attack. The depressing news, together with the increasing anxiety on campus about the proposed tuition increase, has led to big trouble. In fact, we had our first campus confrontation of the year.

At three this afternoon, I was sitting in the "group room"

at U.C.M., waiting for the ten students to arrive for a sensitivity lab.

Suddenly, one of the students burst into the room, caught his breath for a moment, and shouted, "Cutler's been taken!"

Cutler Hall (the main administration building on campus) was occupied; the brief demonstration against the tuition hike was escalating rapidly.

Without really thinking about why or what I was doing, I rushed to Cutler. It was chaos. The crowd seemed to number about two hundred, but I realized with a quick glance that this group was different from the previous militant students I knew: yeah, a few of them were there, but they had been joined by all types—Greeks, jocks, hips, dormies, and all the other labels we conveniently use. In other words, tuition affects everyone.

Most of the action was taking place at the door to the anteroom of the president's office; the action was actually an effort to break through the door. After being jostled in the pandemonium, I found myself wedged between the door and the crowd, and I was shouting, "Stop a minute—cool it—hey, back off a minute—quiet!"

In the semisilence, I suggested that I might be able to get an audience with the president if only the crowd would give me five minutes. With several shouts of antagonism thrown in, the crowd agreed to my request, and everyone sat on the floor.

A campus cop finally let me through the first door, and I told the very pale Dr. Dorf that I would like to talk briefly with President Sowle. I was told that the president was in a meeting with his top advisors. I turned toward the door to the president's office, knocked twice, and heard a voice say, "Come in."

There sat the president—beet-red face, cigar in hand—with his men around a large table. Intense looks of anger in my direction. No one moved.

"President Sowle, could I speak with you for just a moment?"

"I'm sorry, but we're in a meeting."

"But there are about two hundred people outside who are getting ready to come through your door!"

"No."

I left the office immediately, crossed the anteroom as a secretary looked at me fearfully, and entered another office to speak with Vice-President Dorf.

"I *really* have to talk with him."

"He's not going to give in to this sort of student pressure."

"But they only asked to speak with him. They didn't start to get rough until they were ignored. Maybe I can convince him to say just a few words."

"I don't think so."

Back across the anteroom. Knock, knock.

"Come in."

"President Sowle, *please* may I talk with you—just for one minute . . ."

"We are in a mee—"

Before the words got out of his mouth, a very large person grabbed me and threw me out of the office. A small section of the wall had prevented the students from seeing me tossed out. Thank God. Suddenly I realized that the president's aide was calling the state police.

"Dr. Dorf, would you please come out in the hall with me, to talk with the students?"

Outside, Dorf explained amid catcalls that the president would be happy to meet with five representatives of the group in the morning at ten—but not now. Then he added, "Please leave the building; it belongs to the State."

Not a good thing to say to young people who have always been told in school that they *are* the State in a democracy. Yelling followed. I tried again.

"Now look, the guy inside is calling the state police, and they're going to bust your asses! Why don't you just split and find five reps for tomorrow's meeting?"

"We don't have five reps—we're not one group!"

"Okay, then just split before the cops come, and figure something out for tomorrow—you can come back then."

"No, we're staying!"

"Look, Lillian Ramos is dead—let's not screw her memory with this bit."

"That's a goddamned rotten thing to use, Jackson," a coed screamed at me. She was right, but I wasn't ready to admit it.

"The cops are going to be here in about two minutes," I screamed.

Suddenly, the crowd filed out.

I walked, shaking, across the Green to the student center. As I arrived, one of the militants—a navy veteran I knew well —went berserk at me.

"You fucking pig, Jackson, you co-opted us right out of that building!" He shouted in my face for about sixty seconds. When he finished, I quietly said, "Mark, you're full of shit."

I turned and walked back to U.C.M.

January 30

Part two of a bad movie.

This morning at ten, President Sowle met with a group of reporters on radio, for yesterday's group did not send five representatives. Instead, a large group of students milled around the front of Cutler, trying to decide what to do; I tried to convince them to listen to Sowle's comments on the radio before doing anything. My words, of course, were largely ignored.

At about eleven, I heard the sickening thud of a brick breaking glass. The sound caused the crowd to turn away as if by impulse, but, after a few steps, they began heading back, and it was obvious they were there to stay.

Around noon, a window opened in the building, and some guy read a court injunction which informed everyone that they were to get the hell off the Green. Immediately. Fat chance. The crowd grew in size during the next few hours, and no one knew what to do next. That hesitation was short-lived, for the police, in full riot gear, with no badges or name tags, arrived at three, and the total chaos started.

Forty-six arrested.

I caught a nightstick in the ribs.

Lots of people got beat on the head.

Stupidity on all sides.

January 31

I sent a letter to President Sowle, saying that I had tried to be of some help to both sides in a difficult situation. I tried to be a *bridge*, not the enemy.

February 1

Today's Sunday *Messenger* is filled with text and pictures describing the campus turmoil of Thursday and Friday. The pictures are eerie—ten white-helmeted policemen carrying off one student protester, while hundreds of other students look on in shocked passivity—but the chaos and bizarreness of the whole event comes across accurately. Included in the newspaper coverage is an interview with me, excerpts of which follow:

> As much as they were there for the fee issue, I think the students were trying to find out what kind of human being President Sowle is. That was the real issue. They were testing him to see if he was personally interested in them.
>
> The injunction against the protest was effective, in that it left the students legally impotent. It had an incredible psychological

impact. Students see themselves as generally impotent in power politics and law—and the injunction said "you're right."

I don't blame the police who were sent into the situation. That's their job, they're given orders, they go in. In many ways I have real sympathy for them: I see them as occupation troops. But when they are given freedom to act as they will, I will judge them. I cannot fathom how you can hit a human head, a body, with a club.

Again, I have failed to present *all* of my true feelings and thoughts. Of course, I can't give an apology for the behavior of the students, but I know that most of their actions came from increasing frustration with the "powers that be." Even though I have no ultimate defense for them, still more I do not have to make apologies for them.

As the people in the ghetto have learned, so the students are learning: If you want to be heard, you have to make a loud noise, and the loudest noise is often found in the clash with authority figures, be they mayors, police, or federal troops. This unfortunate game was *not* established by the ghetto residents or the students; it was initiated and continues by men who run the system according to their own rules, and the cornerstone of their ruling structure is *power*. It's all astonishingly pathetic and explosive, and no one seems to be trying to change the game.

This afternoon, a few hundred people gathered in Memorial Auditorium for the memorial service for Lillian Ramos. Several speakers, both black and white, offered their views of her life and character. I read a passage from *A Thousand Clowns,* but the most loving, intimate words came from Dr. Harry Chovnick, who had known Lillian for many years.

"Do not make her into a goddess," he sobbed, "for we tear down our goddesses and find new ones . . . she was a large, feeling, black woman who loved the *real* things in life . . . oh, I loved you, Lillian. . . ." Harry openly wept, and I, surreptitiously, with him. What else is there to do with death, except to cry or laugh at it?

King David and Zorba danced.

February 4

Given the feelings in this town about the recent confrontation on the Green, about the words of Spiro Agnew, and about the possibility of future hostilities, it is no wonder that the following entry won first place in the Cub Scout competition on "What America Means to Me":

> I love my country. We have many freedoms. We may go to the church of our choice. We have freedom of speech. This is the land of plenty. We have the highest standard of living of any country in the world. When a person obeys the laws, he will not have any problems.
>
> Larry Lee Ball
> Pack 53
> (from the Athens *Messenger*)

That would have been my letter at that age. But I wonder if anyone will ever tell him what else is going on in his world. Let him have some childhood for now, but someday someone must tell him the truth about Appalachia, the ghetto, urban justice, blackness, and all the rest.

February 6

It is obvious to me now that Tom Niccolls will be leaving. The twinkle in his eyes is too apparent.

If Tom is leaving, then we've got to get some new staff for next year, the more the better. The job is simply getting too big for two of us. We've been talking with the Wesley Foundation about merging with U.C.M.—which would bring their new director, Chuck McCullough, in here—but that machinery appears to grind slowly. I think the Methodists have more committees and bureaucrats than even we Episcopalians have!

The campus ministers met again today—"Come on, now, we really have to get organized."—and I find that I am feeling much closer to the campus rabbi, Joe Polak. He seemed a bit rigid last fall, but he's loosening up rapidly, and I enjoy verbally goosing him now and then.

Joe may well be the only rabbi in the world with the official title of "Minister of the Gospel." You see, when a clergyman arrives in this town, he must get a license to perform weddings legally. Joe went over to the probate court to sign up, and they didn't believe he was a rabbi—he had to have some proof. So there goes Joe, walking down the street, wearing his yarmulke, carrying the framed diplomas like the Tablets, seeking to prove his rabbinate.

Once Joe is finally authorized, there is only one more problem: in Athens, Ohio, rabbis are still an official novelty, it seems, and Joe must accept the license which every "normal" minister gets.

Don't feel too badly, Joe—my license says that I am a minister of the "Episcapol" Church.

February 7

An anonymous letter in the mail:

"Big Man" of the City;
You are sure mighty busy trying to run the O.U. and the city. Most of your "caliber" don't last long, just a passing breeze. We have resided in Athens for over 40 years, and are sure the police have never bothered us, raised our family in what we considered a respectable town, two of our family graduated from O.U., got

their Masters here, and I never heard of the police *abusing* them . . .

February 9

Jude is pregnant! Would you believe it, after all those tests and predictions and concerns and uncertain hopes! God, I'm happy about it.

February 12

Received a rather surprising invitation from Culver Military Academy, my prep school Alma Mater, to speak at a special campuswide conference on ecology, politics, minority groups, etc. I guess there are going to be a few other speakers, including a couple of blacks. Astounding.

I attended Culver for four years, ended up as a gung-ho cadet captain and company commander, and loved most of it. In the senior-class poll of 1960, I placed first in two categories: Most School Spirit and Most Sarcastic. The first "award" was a bit embarrassing but accurate, for the academy provided me with a chance to believe in myself, a feeling which was sorely missing when I first arrived there. The second "award" as a slap at me for my rather compulsive belief in the "system" and my strict intention to "make it." As a line in the academy newspaper once described me, "You can usually find a smile on Tom's face, but don't ever make the same mistake twice in front of him." Maybe I haven't changed much in that regard.

There have been changes, though, and my present beliefs seem to cause surprise to both old and new friends. My classmates at Culver are invariably amazed that I ended up as a "hip priest," and my current friends are equally incredulous when I mention that I attended the academy.

As I remember things, an unusual event happened at Culver during my senior year, an event which remains vividly in my memory.

We all have that moment—don't we?—when the world becomes instantly topsy-turvy, totally different than it was previously, never to be the same again.

I stood at ease along with all of the other cadets at the academy. We were together as a group, standing under the overhanging mezzanine of the immense room in which we ate each meal—the mess hall. We were called to that specific spot on that specific Monday morning to hear a (rumored-important) *message* from our superintendent (even when his messages weren't important, we were duly respectful of the two Air Force stars which gleamed from his shoulders), though there was no advance word on what the subject might be.

To understand the fracture of that moment in my life, the confusion of it, the shock of it, you must understand *how* I stood there. Respectfully. Reverently. With a Republican upbringing. With few doubts about the difference between the good guys and the bad guys. I stood erect, sure, clean, secure. I liked Ike, and Ike would certainly be pleased with me if we ever met; I would stand the same way before him.

The night before this moment, all of us in the corps of cadets had attended a lecture by a visiting speaker, an often-honored writer who spoke on the inhumanity and immorality and illegality of apartheid in South Africa (he had just spent months there), and we were quite overwhelmed by all of it, so we applauded his message with gusto (although he had no stars). We were impressed, we were moved, and we were surprised by some of the happenings in the large world outside our own.

Given that immediate background, given the mental and emotional satisfaction of the previous evening, given the understandings which brought me to stand there in that way, I was not prepared for the message: "Gentlemen, I have just returned to campus, and I find that a known rabble-rouser was here last night. And I hear that he received a standing ovation from you all, from the corps. I am deeply shocked and disappointed. . . ." The two stars gleamed in that stark hall, and he continued the *message* for some minutes, but I didn't hear much of the rest, and it really doesn't matter.

But that was my moment, when the easy pieces weren't fitting in the right slots anymore. I knew that the speaker wasn't a "rabble-rouser" or a "commie," but the two stars said he *was*. Would *everything* I had learned there now have to be reevaluated, rethought, refelt? And, dammit, I *had* been taught some good things within that place—but now I felt betrayed . . .

In the time of Man, that moment was ultimately insignificant. But it was *my* moment of incongruity, despair, growth, and secret joy. A lot of these later years literally grew out of that moment.

I think I'll go back to Culver, to see if I can instigate a few "moments" for others. Maybe things have changed.

February 13

A guy came to the office today to discuss the various issues involved in starting a local "homophile league" for any homosexual students and townspeople who might be interested. He is rightly fed up with the secrecy by which he must live, and he wants to provide an accepting community for others—but I wonder what the response of this local area would be to such an organization. I have a feeling that it wouldn't be too positive, especially in the context of the illegality of homosexuality in Ohio.

I would prefer to have a more casual community of homosexuals, without it looking like a club, for I think that people must have a wider basis for community than simply their sexuality—but perhaps that is simply a cop-out on my part. I guess these people have to start somewhere in their recognition as human beings, and maybe they *do* need some sort of organization to provide an initial motivation.

If a homosexual wants to live that particular life-style—and he or she feels that it is the most beneficial to personal satisfaction as a human being—who am I to say that it is "sick" or "unnatural" or "evil"?

My own behavior in all of this is most frustrating. It seems so symbolic of many difficult questions in my life, things that are neither black nor white. It seems that there are just too many issues crashing in on me, with the demand for me to "take a stand" in the face of my community. I'm starting to think that I'm not strong enough to handle all of these things.

February 15

I have just finished leading a twenty-four-hour "marathon" sensitivity lab, with ten student participants. I am physically and emotionally drained, but it went well, and I was able to deal with some of my own relationships with others as well.

I tend to be rather gregarious in my role in the group. I find that I'm most interested in people who are normally quiet and passive, and I make great efforts to try to open them up a bit, to allow them the opportunity to see that their comments and behavior *can* be acceptable to others. Oftentimes, they get very angry at me for my persistence, but I *persist*. I am convinced that there are really very few people who actually *want* to sit in a corner silently, watching the world pass by in seeming ignorance of their existence. I think that they have to *gain* attention, to reach out at least halfway, for it is a very busy world we have, and it will gladly ignore us unless we say, with some conviction, "Here I am!"

February 18

After a couple of weeks of no response to my letter, President Sowle finally invited me to his office, and we had a talk this afternoon. On the whole, it was good. He seemed to be unusually open to me, admitting his own feelings of anger and resentment when confronted with impossible demands, demands for change over which he had no control—and he knows that the tuition hike is in the hands of the state legislature, not in his office.

I suggested that perhaps the students were unconvinced of his interest in them—although he has done much to show that interest—and that he must be prepared for such "tests" of his priorities. He responded with the observation that he feels particularly uncomfortable with large crowds—he would rather deal with small groups, in which everyone could express their own perceptions. I acknowledged that such a situation might be ideal, but rather unrealistic in the present campus mood. He thanked me for my efforts on January 29, and it was offered sincerely.

I'm not sure that there is any way to "win" in a college presidency nowadays. As I have felt in my own gut, there are simply too many conflicting issues.

February 24

Although we haven't had too many problem pregnancy cases yet this year, I met a very distraught girl this afternoon. She is eight weeks pregnant, the guy involved is black, and one of her more vivid memories of her father is his statement: "If you ever date a nigger, I'll kill both of you!" We talked through the normal options open to a woman—marriage, no marriage, adoption, and, theoretically, a therapeutic abortion —but only the latter seemed realistic to her.

I finally told her that I could not legally arrange an abortion for her, and that I was certainly not a medical expert about the condition of her pregnancy. I gave her the name of an excellent gynecologist in another state, though, and told her that he could probably discuss any legal possibilities with her. I also suggested that she get on the pill at some point if she expected to continue her present relationship. We talked for awhile about her own feelings of guilt, and I thought she had a pretty good grasp of what had happened.

March 5

Tonight I was invited to attend the meeting and "ritual" of the local Methodist sorority, Kappa Phi—and to say a few words. I was surprised with the invitation, first because my growing reputation with the Methodist parish is bad and, secondly, because I am not terribly enthusiastic about "religious fraternal organizations" of any type.

One of my most vivid memories of Jersey is that of offering a "benediction" at a local DeMolay installation of officers. It was incredible! *Endless* words were said about "motherhood" —words which I thought had vanished with the turn of the century. I mean I think it's great if a young man has a healthy, loving relationship with his mother, but that ceremony would have driven Freud right up the wall! I was practically speechless when it came time for the appropriate benediction, and I can't even remember what inane words I mumbled.

So, tonight, I mumbled a few words about commitment to the world, amidst lighted candles and pretty dresses.

On both occasions, I had a fantasy of a wino walking in and

saying, in the middle of the polite ceremony, "I'm looking for Jesus—the guy who said he's willing to clothe me and visit me in jail and listen to my problems—has anyone seen him?"

Too often, I'm afraid, my frustration breeds self-righteousness.

March 8

Just finished leading a marathon sensitivity session over at Procter Center, our first lab composed of *both* students and faculty. Some of the older adults weren't actually faculty, but members of faculty families and so forth.

One girl had previously been to a lab somewhere else, and she drove me batty. She had learned all of the "in" jargon of sensitivity groups, and she laid it on in great scoopfuls.

Something that occurs constantly in such sessions is the discussion of the question, "Who am I really?" I'm tired of that, for it seems to be a convenient evasion of a much more important question: "What am I doing?" It appears to me that I am what I do, as much as that might hurt to admit.

I don't think that there is one single "real me," for I act in a thousand different ways, depending upon my mood and situation. If I act like a bastard at a certain time (and I do!), then the *real me* at that time is a bastard, and it does little to tell myself that the "real me" deep inside is a hell of a nice guy. I might logically ask myself why I'm acting as a bastard at that particular time so that I might change my behavior—but why delude myself?

Is this too Skinnerian? Who cares. It just *is,* that's all. If I am paying my taxes, allowing the war to continue, then I can't tell myself that the real me is loving of humanity. If I say that the real me seeks love and strong relationships, while I sit and stare at my navel constantly, who am I kidding?

Ad infinitum.

It was a good weekend, though, for I had that unique joy of human beings: I learned of some other peoples' lives.

March 11

A very attractive coed came to see me today, ostensibly to discuss her future after graduation. When she removed her coat, though, the room blazed with the obvious: she had on a see-through blouse, and some winning assets were on display. The conversation was inane, and I had the feeling that I was being put through the test which counselors—and particularly clergymen—are given now and then by coy clients. You know, "Are clergymen really human?"

The discussion went nowhere—there were many lengthy pauses (is my breathing getting heavier?)—and the game appeared pretty obvious. As she finally got up to leave, I suddenly said, "Oh, and yes, you have very attractive breasts."

She blushed deeply, and said that she certainly didn't mean to embarrass *me!*

March 15

We are back from the weekend at Culver.

It brought back thousands of memories for Jude and me, and yet things are different. The corps of cadets is restless with many of the confines of the military system (which seems so anachronistic), and I even encountered an underground newspaper which is thriving.

The conference, as such, was handled well, with lots of questions from the cadets, including honest dialogue on current social issues. Any pride I felt was in the academy for allowing this to happen, although I heard a rumor that a member of the board of trustees had called long-distance to find out what on earth was going on at the academy this weekend.

Before I preached in the chapel this morning, I had been invited to come back to the academy next fall to lead a "religious conference." I got the impression *after* my sermon (on the "celebration of life") that my recent invitation back was somewhat regretted. However, some of the faculty I had known were very open and friendly, and that made the trip worthwhile.

Tom Niccolls formally discussed his future resignation at the Board of Managers meeting tonight, and so we started to talk about new staff. I'm a bit uptight—no, *very* uptight—about the process of hiring new members. The relationship with Tom has been so good that I'm afraid of even *looking* for a replacement. I know that the Board is going to leave much of the choice up to me, and that seems to add even more pressure, although I do want that choice of personnel.

It is highly probable that Tom is going to Hiram College in northern Ohio, to be a prof and chaplain. In a way I guess I already resent his fortunate students of next year.

With no brother of my own—and with my father dead—Tom has been many things to me. I love him.

March 20

Most of the students have left the campus for spring vacation, and U.C.M. is quiet.

My concern about the mounting frustration among the students—personally and politically—was confirmed today as I went into the Athens Peace Committee office. A couple of months ago, one of the members painted a large dove on the wall; just recently—as I discovered today—someone has painted a gun underneath the dove.

This represents a change in mood, not so much of the A.P.C. as a group, but of individuals around campus who are coming to believe strongly that this government is incapable of change. The gun, of course, offers the same sort of easy alternative as the U.S. took in Vietnam. And it is "romantic" for numerous fantasies . . .

Someone else has penciled a large X over the gun painting, but I wonder how long it will be before some other person erases the X.

March 29

We have just spent a week at our "farm" in the Catskill Mountains of New York, and what a beautiful interlude it was!

During our stay in the parish in Jersey, we bought the place for monthly escapes from the pressures of the job, and we are presently trying to sell it. With three main buildings, it provides room for about fifteen visitors besides our family. The five acres of land lie about a magnificent mountain stream which is especially full at this time of year. There are some unforgettable memories there, and this visit—probably our last—afforded us a chance to see some old friends, Pat and Scubi, Davis and Esther Ross, as well as the friends from O.U. we took along.

In the middle of the week, Jude and I drove into Manhattan to attend the official declaration of Peter's adoption, and he is now completely ours!

Manhattan was dirtier, noisier, and colder than I had ever remembered it, and we couldn't wait to leave.

Athens seems beautifully homely in comparison . . .

A man went into a forest and asked the trees to provide him a handle for his axe. The trees consented and gave him a young ash. No sooner had the man fitted a new handle to his axe, than he began to use it and quickly felled the noblest giants of the forest. An old oak, lamenting too late the destruction of his companions, said to a neighboring cedar, "The first step has lost us all. If we had not given up the rights of the ash, we might have retained our own privileges and have stood for ages."

—Aesop's Fables

April 7, 1970

The winter feeling in Athens can overwhelm the spirits at times, when the seemingly incessant rain/snow settles on this hilly town, offering short, titillating glimpses of the sun, only to cloud over again in a mockery of our spring hopes. People seek fellowship in warm rooms, trying to ignore the dismal drizzle, but the talk is quieter than that ebullience of last autumn.

The weight of this long, Wales-like season was framed in the sadness of a cemetery today, as I buried the infant son of a young faculty couple. The child had been the stillborn result of great hopes for these sensitive people, for they have previously experienced the confusing reality of miscarriages.

The funeral director, carrying a tiny, white box, led us across the weedy expanse of an uncared-for section of the city cemetery, over near the chain-link fence—the cold, depressing air chilling us beyond the normal iciness of our corporate grief. I offered the Prayer Book words, only because I could think of nothing else, but I knew that even those words were more easily said than believed. I only want to cry with people at such times, to share the empty confusion, not to be the one with the book of magic words.

On the way back to the car, she stopped me for a moment to ask about the possibilities of an adoption: "How long will it take, Reverend Jackson?"

How long will it take for the sun to return?

April 8

Two years ago today, I got my first personal taste of a jail cell, armed intimidation, and urban courts.

It was four days after the assassination of King, after looking into the unbelieving faces of the black people in my parish, after that most recent destructive act upon the continuing leadership of American society.

I went to a Roman Catholic church in the northwest section of Detroit, where about three hundred of us attempted to celebrate a memorial service for the greatest orator of the mid-twentieth century.

After the service, sixty-one of us—including priests, ministers, nuns, housewives, businessmen, and one couple with a three-month-old son—formed a silent vigil on the street opposite the church. We stood there for a few minutes, with the intention of walking silently in single file through the white neighborhood, simply as a reminder of the Memphis (worldwide) tragedy, when—suddenly—there were Detroit police cars on all sides of us.

A man with a bullhorn informed us that we were violating Governor Romney's emergency curfew, which forbade assemblies of more than five persons, although we knew that a silent march of four hundred people had taken place in Grosse Pointe (a wealthy suburb) two days previously with no police intervention at all. Assuming that the curfew was unconstitutional and aimed specifically at the blacks in Detroit, we slowly turned and began our walk. The bullhorn blared a threat of arrest.

I walked second in the long line as we turned the first neighborhood corner, and I could not believe my eyes: there, waiting for us, was an entire platoon of National Guardsmen, in "battle dress," bayonets drawn, some in gas masks, standing next to a large bus with wire mesh over the windows. The bullhorn informed us that we were now under arrest.

All sixty-one people, including the baby, were taken to the local precinct, where we were placed in the service garage. Standing guard over us were four auxiliary policemen, working men who had been given twelve-gauge shotguns for this duty. Each of these men wore a helmet which was obviously his own, decorated with various insignia of personal choice. As we huddled together on the greasy floor, one fellow—a Jew— began to show signs of panic, and I knew why: one of the guards had a small swastika stenciled on his helmet. I began to feel weak and sick to my stomach, wondering just how safe we were in that garage.

After "processing" and some time in the crowded, tiny cells, we were allowed to leave until the next morning, then to the municipal court downtown to be arraigned. The courtroom was packed with police, and there was momentary verbal chaos when the young mother with us decided to nurse the infant— most of the police thought it was disgusting, and I thought it was magnificent.

The judge—black, thank God—mumbled to his bailiff (not intending us to hear) that the curfew was blatantly unrealistic, but we were arraigned one by one. He released us all on personal, thousand-dollar bond, telling us that the cases would come up later on the court calendar.

The cases have never been brought to trial, as far as I know.

My learnings? That I am terrified of such experiences; that I would probably go nuts in that cell if incarcerated for very long; that my whiteness and my collar protect me, even when supposedly breaking the law; that, as I learned previously in the Detroit riots, the police are forced to be "occupation troops" in the cities; that society's laws will be enforced on a geographic and class pattern; that when a black leader is murdered by a white assailant, it is the *blacks* who will pay with loss of fundamental liberties.

Those are heavy learnings for a young, naïve, idealistic priest. I wonder how long they will remain true in the future?

April 14

Tom and I have released a lengthy statement to the *Post* in regard to recent articles on the local homosexual community.

I don't know—the statement sounds like we are hedging, and perhaps we are. *Of course, we are.* It's a cop-out, and I haven't got the guts to call it publicly. If I were a homosexual here, I know damned well that *I'd* want a formal organization, for I would realize that the straights weren't going to bust their butts trying to reform the laws and attitudes.

I'm weak. That's all there is to it. The gospel asks for too much, and I can't give enough. Tonight I had a contractor over to the house to talk about building a large addition—and I know that if I keep opening my big mouth about all these issues, I'm going to get my butt run out of this town. When we left Jersey, I told Jude that I would never again put myself in the position of getting canned—and here we are.

There are too many issues, too many expectations, too many

Bibles making outrageous demands, too many interest groups, too many people. What in the hell is going on?

April 15

A quick trip to Detroit to witness the supposed last legal machinations in the settlement of my father's estate. My mother has been waiting four years while the lawyers and courts have done their thing in this bit, and maybe she'll finally get some results. My dad left a large estate, and I think my mother is terrified of the whole thing—I would be. I never fail to be amazed by the infinite hang-ups of money—there is never the "right" amount—always too much or too little: if you don't have it, you worry about getting it; if you have a lot, you worry about losing it. Incredible.

I think my long hair (not *that* long!) bothered my mother. The lawyers, and all that, but bless her heart, she never really hassles us, and she is willing to listen—always. I just wish I could get her to believe more in herself, to accept her great talents, to know that she is loved by many. But a son can't be a therapist, and I don't have the right to hassle her.

My only sister, Barb, is loony, in a nice way. Daffy. Beautiful. She lives a life-style much different from ours; but she understands and *accepts* my "weird" views for better or worse.

As we sat through the session with the lawyers—honest guys who are actually attempting to help—I could not help but think, though, of that passage in Kurt Vonnegut, Jr.'s *God Bless You, Mr. Rosewater*:

> In every big transaction, said Leech, there is a magic moment during which a man has surrendered a treasure, and during which the man who is due to receive it has not yet done so. An alert lawyer will make that moment his own, possessing the treasure for a magic microsecond, taking a little of it, passing it on. If the man who is to receive the treasure is unused to wealth, has an

inferiority complex and shapeless feelings of guilt, as most people do, the lawyer can often take as much as half the bundle, and still receive the recipient's blubbering thanks.

I blubber a lot.

April 17

Things are starting to heat up on campus again. The situation with the war gets no better, and the students are very aware of that. Tension cuts through the air. Today there was a sizable demonstration against the presence of R.O.T.C. on campus. Nerves are getting frayed, and we are hearing reports of increasing unrest on campuses all over the state . . . all over the country.

The *Post* carried a full-page feature on U.C.M., emphasizing the general views of Niccolls and myself. Out of a long, flattering article, I was interested in the public hearing one specific section:

> "You and I, and everyone I know, have been conditioned to believe that the beauty of a cathedral is more important than any human life."
>
> Jackson says the response of Jesus to this was: "It ain't so."
>
> "There's a drunk lying on the couch downstairs. If I say he isn't as beautiful as a cathedral, I'd better hang it up. It might be more important to have a group of tourists to take a tour through *him*."

April 21

Miami University students staged a "flush-in" today, as a protest act in regard to the growing tension on that campus. Everyone in the dorms flushed the toilets at the same time, causing a tremendous loss in the city water pressure for a few hours. Well, at least it wasn't "violent." If things are getting to that point on a campus as "quiet" as Miami, then it's time to start chewing nails here in Athens.

I hear, by the way, that the U.C.M. on that campus is catching hell for allowing its mimeograph machine to be used by the "radical" students. Ahh, it's nice to have company in the religious doghouse.

April 22

About three weeks ago, I told a large group of militant students that I didn't want to hear about it if any of them were planning an "action" anywhere—for two reasons: first, I would probably feel compelled to talk them out of it, and they wouldn't listen to me anyway; and secondly, the whole bit about "clergy privileged communication" is not legally binding; that is, I can be legally required to testify against a "client" in a court of law. If I didn't, I would face a contempt-of-court ruling. They must have taken me seriously, for today's events were previously unknown to me.

In the midst of the Earth Day activities, eight female students and one male student—all of them close acquaintances of mine—were involved in a sit-in during an R.O.T.C. class, and all of them were busted. There are, of course, conflicting statements as to what happened in the class, but that seems to make little difference now.

I suppose that I should be very upset about this breach of the law. I'm not. If we can destroy another nation—as we are doing—with immunity, then I refuse to apologize for this action by these young people. They did not hurt anyone; when they demonstrated peacefully in Washington last November, their president purposely ignored them (and three hundred thousand others); when they write letters to the government, they receive form letters in return. Let us not continue to tell them to "eat cake."

At five this afternoon, one of the ecology-group leaders called me, demanded to know why *I* had planned the R.O.T.C. sit-in, and suggested that the event had "ruined the entire Earth Day." It hadn't—but I could understand how angry he felt about the surprise of it all. There are simply too many issues in this crazy world, and I'm beginning to wonder if they won't all blow at once.

April 27

Things are getting heavy. Debates, arguments, frustration. Everyone seeking ways to release the growing pressure. No power base or influence on government in these lives, so reason often seems unreasonable. Last night, in a sort of "rite-of-springtime" atmosphere, there was dancing in the streets and numerous bonfires.

I don't know where we are headed.

April 30

Wherever it is, it doesn't look pleasant now. Our president just made it a brand new ball game.

I have absolutely no understanding of Richard Nixon's sensitivity or intelligence now, for he has just announced that he is sending American "support" for an allied invasion of Cambodia. If he *wanted* to ignite a domestic bomb, he couldn't have thought of a better way to do it. The mood of the people I saw tonight was terribly hostile, and the campus is frighteningly alive with debate and slogans.

Joe Polak and I joined a couple of other panelists on a radio show tonight, ostensibly dealing with religious questions, but the calls into the studio evidenced much different questions. One caller informed us that there were some more bonfires outside, and wondered why we were not "putting out the fires and quieting the students." We said that we doubted our persuasive abilities at this point, for Nixon's words were much more obvious than anything we could say. The caller was incensed by our response, of course, but I do not feel obliged this evening to rationalize the obscenity of our president's action.

The situation at Ohio State is becoming very difficult, and we receive constant reports on the campus turmoil there.

On our campus late this evening, the scene has become chaotic, with water balloons being hurled at one of the trustees (a man who manages to patronize the students everytime he addresses them), with fistfights breaking out between the "hips" and the "jocks." It is ugly, frightening.

A late newscast says that there are disturbances in Cleveland, at Miami University, and at Kent State.

IV

> It was the best of times, it was the worst of times, it was the age of wisdom, it was the age of foolishness, it was the epoch of belief, it was the epoch of incredulity, it was the season of Light, it was the season of Darkness, it was the spring of hope, it was the winter of despair, we had everything before us, we had nothing before us, we were all going direct to Heaven, we were all going direct the other way.
>
> —Charles Dickens,
> A Tale of Two Cities

May 1, 1970

Word comes via radio and television and newspapers that campuses all over the country are erupting hourly into scenes of desperate protest against Nixon, racism, the draft, and student powerlessness. In Ohio, most of the action seems to be centered at Ohio State and Kent State—which surprises me, for I considered both to be very conservative campuses. Maybe they are—maybe this new frustration is overwhelming *everyone.*

May 4

It is now very late at night on the longest day I have experienced in many years.

There are at least four students dead at Kent State.

Dead.

I am tired and hungry and depressed and confused and scared and empty.

The news of the Kent bloodbath arrived here around one this afternoon. Amidst the disbelief, I gathered the rest of the staff, plus two other campus ministers, and we tried to decide on some public response. But what is there to say in the face of this ultimate obscenity, this trigger for more violence, this insane act against a young, protesting society? We decided that our only answer could be: "We refuse to join in the killing!"

A Niccolls' call to Cutler Hall informed the administration that we were planning to stage a three-day "fast" on the College Green, that we hope to stabilize the campus mood rather than aggravate it. Dorf was less than enthusiastic with our plan, but he did not block it. I wonder if he has forgotten his comments of last summer about the ministry acting as a "bridge"? I can't knock him though—he's probably as scared as we are.

No one really knows what to do here, but everyone knows that the chances for wider violence and loss are strong. So there is a pervasive effort to keep communication—any communication—open between the thousands of wandering souls in this place. Our site for the fast—under a gigantic, beautiful tree in the middle of the Green—has attracted many visitors, who come to discuss the latest news or to sit silently on our numerous blankets.

The tired slogan of "Bring the War Home" has now taken on a sickening aspect . . . four hearts have stopped. How do we respond to all of this—what sort of "religious" or "Christian" or "Jewish" response does one make at this point? Here we are, about forty years combined experience in the ministry, with backgrounds in campus work, inner-city work, suburban parishes, and administration, and yet the same question haunts each of us: *What now?*

The mood on campus is utter confusion. Can students really be shot to *death* in a protest? What are the "radicals" going to do? Will the university remain open? Does anyone have any suggestions about *anything?*

We will try the "fast" thing—I wonder if people will merely laugh at us? But laughter is better than gunfire.

"Happy are those who hunger and thirst for justice, for they will be satisfied." So says our sign on the tree near our site. I hope so.

The Kent deaths are beginning to sink into peoples' brains and guts, and there is an unstated fear. I need people around me now—Jude, Niccolls, Polak, Craig—hundreds of people who will huddle in close hope—with no raps on "doctrine" and no hassles on "membership"—if we are not *one,* then we shall be consumed by hate.

I keep thinking of the words by Jack Newfield at the end of his book on Robert Kennedy: "Maybe we have so completely alienated one another that we will *not* overcome. We must make it work. We are under such massive judgement."

A Gallup Poll released today suggests that 51 percent of the American public approves of Nixon's Cambodian move. *I wonder where those people are*—I haven't talked with any of them recently.

I heard Nixon's statement on Kent: "This should remind us all again that when dissent turns to violence it invites tragedy." You had better find out who did the shooting, Mr. President.

There was a magnificent rally on the Green tonight, with at least four thousand people—all kinds of people. It was gentle and abrasive and loving and hostile—it was a collection of all the thoughts and emotions which continue to whirl in this place. A coed from Kent gave an impassioned plea for nonviolence, which met with widespread applause but some disagreement.

I noticed that Rabbi Polak was near the microphone, and suddenly there was a loudspeaker request for Jackson and

Niccolls to come forward. My heart began to beat rapidly—
I felt embarrassed and quite useless—and I joined the others
on the jerry-built stage. Joe Polak gave a moving, personal
prayer, emphasizing the human waste at Kent, suggesting the
possibility of humane responsiveness here. Tom Niccolls followed with a short prayer, as only Tom can say it.

As the microphone was handed to me, I discovered that I
could see very few of the four thousand faces, for the arc lights
flooded the stage with a brilliant barrier. But I could *feel* what
was going on—there was the silence of hesitation, the uncertainty of response—the general embarrassment of a few ministers being given a brief opportunity to say something of
value and persuasion. I could barely perceive the pauses in
my heartbeat—where am I and what am I doing? Is this really
the aftermath of death, or do I look through that light screen
upon a rock concert? Is Cambodia a reality, or have I been
transformed by a dream into a Billy Graham crusade for the
"American way of life" in some southern city?

Reality—and I speak:

> I've gotta try one more time . . . I just want a moratorium for
> *one day* on the terms "jock" and "Greek" and "hippie" and
> "yippie" and all those things we use to punch each other out . . .
> I heard a Kent State student on the radio this afternoon say that
> he thought the National Guard was using blanks until he saw a
> girl's head blow open. . . . It's time to quit blowing open heads
> and disgusting each other. . . . Can't we just *once* do it? Just
> *one day,* that's all I ask. . . . Please remember that head that
> was blown open. . . . Do something embarrassing tonight. . . .
> Like don't kill each other. Like touch someone. . . . Be a fool,
> for gentleness is foolish in these present days. . . . Jesus, it's so
> hard to be together at a time like this. . . . Amen.

As I handed the microphone to someone nearby, the applause began and grew thunderous and prolonged. I couldn't
handle it. Like Tom Niccolls on October 15, I ran to the back
of the crowd to hide myself, to escape the very embarrassment

and affection which I had just beckoned! But I couldn't handle it—and I cried hard—and I still want to cry.

The rally seems to have set a positive mood for the time being—at least violence has been rejected for awhile, and other avenues are being explored. A two-day strike has been called, and tomorrow holds numerous demands.

I am very tired. The adrenaline has given way to the absence of food. I am very tired.

May 5

People crowd the campus Green, although I don't know how effective the strike is. Another long, long day, filled with such various and conflicting emotions—every minute is packed with personal demands from dozens of "interest groups" and university personnel. My growing hunger for food is being matched by my hunger for at least five minutes of privacy and silence.

President Sowle addressed a large rally today, and he was human and honest, I thought. It was obvious throughout his appearance at the rally that a majority of students are looking to him as a surrogate father—their own parents are miles away, and they need to see the reaction—in person—of the "older generation." Sowle is often so formal in his appearance —no, I guess it's more "authoritarian" than formal—authoritarian in the sense that everyone knows that he is "the man," the one who will make the necessary decisions, for better or worse. At one point today, he agreed to put on a red armband, and the student response was overwhelmingly positive. I wonder how many of their fathers would have done that! He's trying very hard to keep things sane here, and he must be aware that one major mistake could end the whole effort.

Gordon Parks, the brilliant black photographer and writer, arrived in town today to deliver a speech to the College of

Communications, a speech which was planned months ago. I went over to the University Inn late in the afternoon to speak with him, to apprise him of the situation on campus, to ask him if he would speak to a large rally tonight. He agreed to speak, of course, and his concern for the whole situation was apparent. He gave that motel room an aura of importance, and yet he seemed a bit out of place in its perfect, colonial decoration. He is a strong man with a complexion which shows the lines of battles and victories which were so finely described in his *A Choice of Weapons.* The face also showed deep fatigue, and I regretted the request for his appearance at the rally, but I felt that he would be a strong influence for positive action. It was an honor for me to be with him.

As the gym floor was packed with every type of student—a few thousand strong—I gave a short introduction for Gordon Parks, and the students were wild in their enthusiasm for his presence there. He spoke briefly of the catastrophe at Kent and of the war situation, ending with: "As John Kennedy said, those who make peaceful revolution impossible will make violent revolution inevitable. I will say to Mr. Agnew and to Mr. Nixon that if you don't stop the killing in Vietnam and Cambodia and on campuses, then you're going to have the *damndest* revolution!"

The rally continued for the next hour amid the noise of rhetoric, debate, applause, and anxiety. Some plans were made for tomorrow, plus a few announcements. The leaders of the protest movement seemed a bit frustrated over the ineffectiveness of the strike, and they know, I'm sure, that several thousand students would go to class even if the Kent murders had happened here.

Parks' speech is juxtaposed with a statement I heard on the radio after the rally, a statement issued by Maj. Gen. Winston P. Wilson, Jr., the Pentagon chief of National Guard affairs: "Those guys were given a job of restoring law and order. That's what they were called for. They were doing their job as best they can." That is correct—and that is exactly the point of this entire protest, General Wilson. They were doing a job as best they could, and that resulted in four deaths and many injuries. I remember the National Guard in Detroit during the 1967 disturbances—I remember the events around the "Algiers Motel incident"—I remember the incredible lack of training of those young men, the realization in their own faces that they were not sufficiently prepared to deal with civilian emergencies. Tragically, they did a job as best they could, and that is as unfair to them as it is to those they face.

I suppose that the one very good piece of news today is that Gov. James Rhodes is apparently losing his primary bid for the U.S. Senate to Robert Taft, Jr. I think the Rhodes administration can be remembered in history for two things: the handling of the Kent State situation, and that he named tomato juice as the "state drink" of Ohio.

May 6

The first sign of violence came early this morning. An R.O.T.C. supply room was fire-bombed, leaving about twenty-five-hundred dollars in damages. I wonder how many Vietnamese villages were napalmed this morning, leaving *human* destruction. The fire here is the first indication of "uncontrolled" action. It could have an opposite effect, though—it might quiet down some people. Who knows?

About three thousand people joined in a "March against Murder"—silently walking through town, a drum beating the sound of a dirge. It was an amazing sight, for the march was joined by many townspeople for the first time, as well as the Hare Krishna religious sect from West Virginia. Beforehand, Niccolls and I had an argument with some of the more militant students who wanted to stage a massive sit-in at the major intersection near the Green. We finally agreed to let each group make its own decisions, although we argued against an escalation of tactics at this point. Consequently, as the march ended back on the Green, about sixty of the militants sat down in the street for awhile, and they were finally influenced to leave.

I find it ironic that we are debating nonviolent tactics here, while Nixon and his boys continue to destroy human lives at will. Even when we try to direct attention to the war, that attention gets diverted right back here.

The scene on the Green has been positive on the whole, and it is a great comfort to me to be with a community of people who are trying very hard to be open with each other. At the "fast site" this afternoon I talked with a young man who said that he had always revered Richard Nixon—in fact, he had a huge poster of Nixon hanging on his dormitory wall. Last night, he shredded the poster into hundreds of pieces. This young guy was quiet and reflective, and I knew that he felt terribly betrayed.

Our heroes fall daily, if not by assassins' bullets, then by their own actions. There is a pervasive feeling that no one is "in charge" of this nation, but I shudder to think of the consequences if we as a people start demanding complete "control."

I hear via the administrative grapevine that Jolly Jim Rhodes is really putting the pressure on Sowle and other university presidents to close down the various schools at the "first sign of trouble." Sowle is obviously working his butt off to keep this place functioning, and I hope at this point that he doesn't give in.

The fast ends tomorrow at noon, and I'm starting to feel very weak.

May 7

At noon we broke the fast with bean soup and homemade bread. It was glorious to taste food again, even after only three days without. Forgive me, dear Asians, for my gluttony today, for my easy return to middle-class life, for my inner satisfaction that I am not in your positions. Forgive me my hypocrisy in the face of your own desolation. I got the smallest fraction of understanding of your hunger in the past three days, and my own weakness in the midst of it was a shock to my normally comfortable life.

Bob Hughes was correct in saying that the only reason to fast is for the expectation of breaking the fast in a new understanding of oneself and one's world. If there was a celebration to break-fast, it was in the realization that no one has yet died in *this* place. Perhaps our "foolish" acts of fasting and communion and singing and being together helped keep the scene a bit stable. But as we spend our energies in maintaining the stability of this place, we simply allow the Cambodian obscenity to continue.

We sent a telegram to Nixon, signed by three thousand students, faculty members, and townspeople. I'm sure that it's four hundred dollars down the drain, but there doesn't seem to be much else to do. Is there something else?

The large student population of blacks made its first impact this afternoon, and it was a heavy one. Since Monday, the blacks have remained on the sidelines of the rallies and demonstrations, and the white student leaders have been a bit too self-conscious to ask for black involvement. I mean by that that the white students don't really know what the black students want in all of this. I think that the blacks are more concerned with the adverse treatment they receive in this town than with the chaotic war situation—but I may be wrong about that.

The blacks made their presence felt this afternoon, though. Four hundred strong, they went to the main street in Athens and quietly told each store owner to close up shop for the rest of the day. Most of the owners complied—one woman was allowed to keep her store open—and they were angry, scared, and resentful of the event. Many of the Court Street businessmen control other aspects of student life, such as housing units, and they don't like the idea of being intimidated. They can, of course, treat the students with condescension, but when the tables are turned, there is hate. It was a touchy situation, but I am inwardly pleased that the blacks did it. I don't think that the merchants will ever forget this day.

This ironically is our week for the U.C.M. fund-raising campaign, and I'm sure that the merchants will not be filling our coffers after today, for we are naturally blamed in part for anything that any of the students do "wrongly." We've already got about four thousand dollars pledged from people out of town, and about two thousand five hundred dollars from those in Athens, so things look pretty good anyway. I hear that one merchant—who receives somewhere around five hundred dollars worth of U.C.M. business each year—has offered to donate *two dollars*. Ah, the Lord loves a cheerful giver.

The debate of violence versus nonviolence seems to increase with every hour, for few alternatives are being developed for the channeling of frustration. Early this evening a throng of students emerged from the Green onto Court Street, and the tension was high. The police acted very well and calmly, but the beads of perspiration were apparent on many foreheads. Everyone merely milled around, as if waiting for some catalyst to act, but nothing violent happened. In fact, it was probably the first time this year that I have seen the students and police talk openly with each other. In that sense it was positive, but I didn't especially like the overall feeling.

I guess we're not alone in our anxiety and frustration, though—I heard on the radio tonight that there are approximately 227 schools which have closed down in one way or another. We are functioning here, and that is an oddity, at least in the state of Ohio.

May 8

Two big mistakes were made today, and if they are not rectified, we might as well close up shop.

The students who were involved in the R.O.T.C. sit-in on April 22 were arraigned (or something like that) this morning, and Judge Sheeter increased each bond to five hundred dollars, thereby forcing the students back into jail. It is simply incredible that the man would have that little sensitivity to the tension in this place. That provides just the "issue" that is needed by the supermilitants to provoke a confrontation.

In mid-afternoon, as Tom Niccolls and I were walking toward the Green, Captain Cochran motioned to us to come over to his police cruiser. I couldn't imagine what was going on, but Tom and I climbed in the back seat. Another officer was driving the car, as Cochran sat in the front passenger seat and talked to us. He said that he understood the tension surrounding the Sheeter decision, and that he would personally talk with Sheeter about the possibility of reducing the bonds again, but he wanted it known that he would personally "throw the book" at the students if they broke any more laws. It was apparent that Cochran disliked us and the students involved, but I knew that he was extremely uptight about the chances for nighttime violence. I have no idea how far Cochran will get with Sheeter, but I find it interesting that this is the first time this year I have heard such an offer from the "power structure." Now that there is some "student power" on the line, we might be able to negotiate out of this one.

The second mistake is almost a cliché of administrative bureaucracy. This afternoon, after President Sowle left for Washington to accept an invitation from Howard K. Smith to appear on the evening news, an edict was sent out of Cutler Hall, informing the students that the loudspeaker system was no longer available on the Green. I went to Cutler immediately to speak with Vice-President Dorf about it, and I was told that it was no longer "appropriate" to have the loud-speaker, that the students could communicate in small groups or use the university xeroxing equipment to copy handbills. I suggested that this was an extreme error, for our continued functioning was predicated on the ability of the students to feel a sense of community, to openly debate and discuss the various possibilities of dissent. I lost the argument.

This evening, Sowle appeared on the ABC news hour, answering questions from Smith, proudly announcing that O.U. was one of the few universities still operating in Ohio and adding: "A marvelous thing has happened at O.U. There has been a joining of ranks by practically everybody to keep the university open. This may be Ohio University's finest hour!" But back here in Athens, our "finest hour" was drawing short, for the students knew—even as Sowle spoke—that the co-operation was ending. I will choose to believe that Sowle didn't know about the speaker-system decision before he left for Washington.

Tom Niccolls has met with a large group of people who are working hard to keep communication open, and they have planned to go to Columbus to meet Sowle's plane, to lay out the situation for him, and to make a few "forceful" suggestions. Someone has got to do something quickly. The debates on violence/nonviolence have gone on too long, Nixon has said too much on television, there is no communication from

Washington, and small incidents of hostility are becoming evident. Many students keep asking me to keep the campus peaceful, as if my words at this time would have some great effect. The absurdity of the speaker-system decision has shown the students that we ministers have very little clout with the Cutler Hall gang, and I cannot magically change that.

Today's Gallup Poll: 57 percent of the public approves of the Cambodia "incursion" (read "declaration of war") but only *if it works!* Our morality, it seems, is now a matter of success and body counts. Explain *that* to the students, O Great Nix.

May 9

Nixon provided the perfect symbol of the agony and anxiety of this nation this week, when he spoke to some demonstrators in Washington: "Try to understand what we are doing. Sure, you come here to demonstrate. Go shout your slogans on the Ellipse. That is all right. Just keep it peaceful."

We *do* understand what you are trying to do, Mr. President!

We are ashamed of what you are trying to do.

Why should we continue to spend countless hours in our efforts to "keep it peaceful" when you act illegally in Cambodia? How can you ask us to strain for peaceful assembly while you kill thousands of *people* everyday, trying to "save face"?

Niccolls and the group met Sowle's plane, told him of the current situation, and suggested that classes be canceled on Tuesday (May 12) so that the community could openly discuss the alternatives. He said that he would consider the situation.

Things are breaking down. People are being divided into enemy camps, nerves are laid bare, and there has been too little sleep for everyone. Nixon is assuming that the public is

behind him, and the students know that they are being ignored. Cutler Hall wants to keep the university open, but they
are acting as though we can simply go back to business as
usual. Those various differences in attitude add up to trouble,
and we all know it.

I sent a brief note to Captain Cochran, thanking him for
his efforts in the past couple of days, for Sheeter decided to
rescind the increase in bonds.

May 10

Mistakes three and four: Sowle has decided not to cancel
classes on Tuesday (no one will listen to *that* peace group
again!) and he and/or his administrative assistants have denied a request from another student group to allow two speakers—one of them John Froines of the Chicago Seven—to
speak here tomorrow night. It seems that the "cost" would be
too much for the university to handle. I think that if they deny
this request, the "cost" to this community may be larger than
anyone imagines. There is simply too much up for grabs right
now, and a few more arbitrary decisions will bring the whole
house down . . .

May 11

Why do FBI men always look so much like FBI men? I
was visited today by the new agent in town, and I could have
picked him out of a crowd of a thousand people. Does Hoover
really want to keep the stereotype alive? Well, we had an interesting talk which accomplished very little, although I did
discover that the FBI must see me as the "Hoodlum Priest"
or something similar, for the agent was absolutely positive

that I knew *everything* in the political "underground" of Athens!

"Could you tell me who firebombed the R.O.T.C. supply room, Reverend Jackson?"

"No, I really don't know."

"Could you make a reasonable guess?"

"Sorry, but that seems a bit unfair."

"Do you know who is taking parts off of the R.O.T.C. vehicles?"

"No, I didn't know anyone was doing that."

"Do you know of any plans to cause disruptions here?"

"No, but I would imagine that things could get hot if students feel that their opinions on the war are being totally ignored."

The discussion went on like that for several minutes, and I appreciated the fact that Don Craig was sitting (nervously) in the office with us—I wanted a witness badly. Finally, the gentleman closed his briefcase, straightened his J. Edgar Hoover suit, and departed amidst cordial smiles. I wonder if all of that went into my file?

John Froines finally got his chance to speak tonight in the gym—the administration changed its mind—and it was a rather anticlimactic event. Froines said all of the same things we've been talking about for a week, and he spent most of his time discussing the situation with the Black Panthers in New Haven. That is important, yes, but we are trapped on a tightrope of emotion and frustration *here*—I guess that I looked to him for the same sort of magic which has been asked of me in the past week, and that's crazy. Some guy from the "White Panther" group in Michigan followed Froines at the mike, and he was deadly dull, so we left.

Later this evening, about 150 students "took over" Chubb Library, a vacant building on the Green which has not been used since the new Alden Library was opened. I had been home for a few minutes after the rally, when Don Craig called to give me the news. I immediately went over to Chubb, but I realized that there was little I could do.

The students say that they want the building to be a center for student activities—they had made this request earlier this week—but, as usual, the administration has different plans. It was a pathetic scene tonight, for the students are occupying an empty building, and that will simply become a point of confrontation. But perhaps it is all inevitable, what with the stagnation of ideas and possibilities here. Rabbi Polak was in and out of the building several times, in an effort to create some dialogue, but to no avail.

There were several students outside of Chubb yelling counterslogans and counterobscenities at the students inside, and that is another example of the growing hostility. I suppose that frustration leads to internecine battles, perhaps only because there is nothing else to battle—the "enemy" is invisible.

I had nothing to offer at Chubb tonight—I stood by a tree and passively observed the whole bizarre event. I have run out of things to say or do—instead of ideas to present, I only react to the current situation, and that sort of thing cannot go on forever.

I'm going to bed.

May 12

Early this morning, the police surrounded Chubb Library, the students were informed of their "trespassing," and the students left. No confrontation. A nonevent. More frustration. No new ideas. Growing edginess. Lack of sleep.

Also early this morning, the recently completed Nelson Cafeteria was fire-bombed. About $120,000 in damages they say. But the damage goes beyond that: there is now a pervasive discussion on campus of the implications of violence. Some students are saying that violence is violence only if it is against a *person,* that acts against property are okay. Others are saying that demonstrators should be shot as they were at Kent.

People are going to classes. People are sitting around the student center. People are talking.

Everyone is waiting, it seems, for that "something" to happen.

May 13

I think that the "final" mistake has been made.

Because of the Chubb Library incident, the university administration, with the acceptance of the trustees, has officially suspended seven students, in each case saying that "the continued presence of the student on campus constitutes a clear and present danger to the orderly functioning of the University community."

The "mistake" in all of this is actually a matter of two aspects: first, the suspensions were delivered to the students in the middle of last night, thereby giving the impression of "gestapo" techniques—and that sort of news travels fast; secondly, of the seven students involved, one of them, a young guy named Neil, is clearly one of the most *un*dangerous human beings in this area of the country! Everyone knows that he plays the role of the clown most of the time, and it is patently absurd to portray him as a "threat" to this community.

Tonight, in the midst of confusion and paranoia, the first real confrontation took place. A couple hundred students congregated at the main intersection, a brick went through a bookstore window, and the tear gas flew. Along with Tom Niccolls and a few others, I was standing at the corner, trying to keep things orderly—and it didn't work. It was my first real taste of tear gas, and I don't think I want another one.

In the midst of the chaos, a young man I know had a seizure. I tried to get him some help. At the same moment, one of the "Jesus freaks" confronted me and asked me if I wanted to *pray*. With the tear gas overwhelming me I responded, "No, I want to vomit." He disappeared—I suppose to find another sinner.

The Green area was emptied after an unmarked police car came swerving down the street, back doors open, tear gas gushing out from a large pump on the back seat. A real weapon. It worked.

My eyes still hurt and my skin burns. I'm tired. To hell with it.

Incessantly, my mind and gut feud over the violence/non-violence issue, and I've forgotten which arguments can be listed on either side of the question. Inwardly, I am a violent pacifist . . . outwardly, I am simply confused. Understand? To hell with it.

May 14

All the actors knew their roles tonight, and we acted them out perfectly. The ultimate confrontation arrived, with bigger and better tear gas, more and more bricks. The police played their role with relish and more sophisticated equipment. The students acted in the roles of urban guerrillas, facing the gas, falling back, regrouping, going again. A frightening thing to watch.

Everyone was expecting it, and preparations were made by all sides. The police mounted gas-grenade launchers on the top of a Court Street store. The students prepared water buckets to wash out eyes. One of the dorms on College Street looked like a scene from "Gone with the Wind," with its white columns and "first aid" sign, and pretty young women. The stage was set, and the actors rehearsed their lines.

In the middle of it, we got a call from the advisor in Howard Hall, a girl's dormitory, saying that the gas was so heavy there that they wanted to evacuate the building and bring the sixty girls to the U.C.M. building. I agreed. With the girls stashed in the basement, I went to the first-floor lounge to discover that several of the more militant male students had come into U.C.M. I told them that they would have to leave, but they countered with the rumor that a curfew had been established, and they would certainly be arrested if they went outside. I told them to sit down on the floor and stay out of trouble. I went back upstairs to talk with Don Craig, when suddenly there was an uproar from the first floor. I ran down, looked out the window, and realized that an auxiliary policeman was standing on the front porch, getting ready to throw a gas grenade through the front window. Don and I quickly went out the door to face the guy.

"Can I help you?"

"I want those radicals in there!"

"What for?"

"I want 'em—they're guilty of tearing up this town!"

"I'm sorry, but we have sixty girls in the basement, and I can't afford a major disturbance in there—I'm afraid the girls might panic."

At this point, Don went back inside to call for help in getting the girls out of U.C.M. and to get this guy off of our porch. I continued the porch "discussion."

"I'm going to get those guys if I have to gas this place!"

"I think that would be very unwise. I think many people might get hurt for nothing. I don't know if those men did anything or not, but I'm not letting you storm this house . . ."

As the guy raised his arm, threatening to throw the gas canister, he yelled, "You ministers are behind seven-eighths of our problems in this town . . . I've lived here for a long time and I know who the troublemakers are . . ."

"Could I have your name or badge number please?"

"You don't need to know my name . . . you just need to know that I've lived here a lot longer than you have!"

"I don't really think we're going to get anywhere this way." I went back inside, expecting the canister to follow me, but the guy just stood on the porch, threatening with his arm. Someone came from the university to get the girls, and one of the militant guys tried to stop them, saying that they would get busted if the girls left. Thankfully, one of the girls slapped him across the face, and they all left.

Eric, a huge senior who had been with me all evening, decided to leave. He said that he was going to crawl home on his stomach. I hope he made it.

A few minutes later, two regular policemen in gas masks came to the front door and told the guy with the canister to "forget it," and he went off with them.

The whole thing scared the hell out of me, and I am still shaking. I don't know what else I could have done, but I'm not sure I did the "right" thing. God, I'm tired of all of this. Where is Cambodia now? Where are the four Kent students? Was the Cambodian venture worth all of this—three hundred campuses filled with tear gas, people hating each other, police cars destroyed, hundreds of people injured?

I can't stop shaking.

May 15

At three o'clock this morning, President Sowle officially closed the university, and the mayor has called in the National Guard.

Soldiers now line our streets.

There was too much in the past week to discuss—too many

unanswered questions—too many mistakes by all of us. But everyone lost today. The rocks and the tear gas added up to a circus of loss, and no one wins.

Everyone is tired and going home.

It's hard to say good-bye to people after we just started to say hello last week.

There is going to be hell to pay in this town.

Given Nixon's announcement of April 30, I wonder what else could have happened.

God, it's all so scary.

V

Never, "for the sake of peace and quiet," deny your own experience or convictions.

—Dag Hammarskjöld

May 17, 1970

A very quiet town—on the surface.

Tear gas lingers in the air on Court Street. Housewives and children squint and wipe their eyes on the way to Woolworth's or school. Every citizen has reason to reflect angrily on the martial atmosphere of this once serene Appalachian area. Soldiers, smoke, angry looks, busy gossip: a surrealistic landscape.

Two are dead and several injured at Jackson State. It is a judgment on me that I was not particularly shocked by that incident; I have come to *expect* the deaths of black people in the South—and the North. That expectation is disgusting, for it makes me less sensitive to life. I didn't expect *white students* to be killed, so Kent was a bolt of surprising fear crashing into my little world. Had the Jackson State murders happened during the middle of last week, the catharsis, I think, would have left this place in shambles.

The underlying resentment here—the new "gospel of revenge"—is probably best stated in a column which appeared in today's Sunday *Messenger*. It is written by a woman who writes a weekly column, although she lives several miles from Athens. Herewith, "Have Commies Won First Round?" by Beulah Jones:

It looks very much as though the Communists have won the first round in America in the battle of democracy versus a dictatorship.

A so-called "handful" of radical students have closed colleges, depriving serious students of their right to education, one of the precepts of the Constitution spelled out by the early patriots.

This has been one of the important aims of the Communists— to cut off knowledge. A misinformed or ill-informed people make good Communists.

With the help of militant youth; well-meaning(?) ministers who advocate peace at any price, even to giving in to the Communist demands; a few red-fringed faculty members; permissive parents and a permissive society; lack of respect for anyone including the law, even from members of Congress; the boys who want to be treated as men but do not want a man's job of protecting his country; all have contributed to the spectacle of seeing a free nation be absorbed by an aggressive nation.

America's line of defense has been so denuded that we will shortly be at the mercy of Communists unless there is a change in attitudes. They rolled over Poland and Hungary with tanks. They don't need to here. They never planned to.

Students and all youth who do not want education or a vocation nor defend the country should be given a place where they can pursue other means of expressing themselves! One where they can't be seen nor heard.

The demonstrators would have America settle for defeat! America should be so strong that we would have peace, but we are being paralyzed by lefties, peaceniks, rioters and the like.

In World War II we won a war with two battlefronts because Americans were joined against the enemy. The Red Propagandists have overlooked no avenue—schools, churches, mass media, cultural areas, any place in America.

Taxpayers should know that this year in the United Nations, America helped finance the 100th Birthday Anniversary of one Vladimir Ulyanov, better known as Lenin, founder of Bolshevik Communism. His concept of education is, in his words, "not a single problem of the class struggle has ever been solved in history except by violence."

The great cry in America—free food, free housing, free education, free salary, free everything, will spell the end of American freedom if the government persists in trying to supply the wants and needs and desires of its people. Some initiative should be left to the individual, at least to be his own judge of whether he wishes to be rich or poor.

If America sinks her battleships, destroys her planes, tanks and guns, who will keep the enemy at bay while the marchers march? Let them try parading in Moscow.

The good children in this land should not have to be cowed by unthinking parents who feel that their children should be free to spoil life for others. Perhaps what we need is a group of really angry women with hatchets and umbrellas to clean things up. They have done it before. I have been told there aren't soap boxes anymore so I'm standing on a good old fashioned cheesebox!

Hatchets and umbrellas! Is this the same angelic voice which has been telling young people to act "responsibly" in the past? And, of course, we have another example in Beulah of the same old routine: If you don't like it here, go to Moscow!

Another brief article in today's paper is meant to be "humorous" I suppose, but it appears to me to be of a more sinister nature than even Beulah's. It is headlined, "Peaceful Protest Comes in Small Package":

The idea of peaceful protest to win an issue and the capitulation of a school administration has spread into an Athens Elementary school.

While college students were protesting on the campus, four third grade pupils decided to mimic their elders and voice their dissatisfaction with things in their class.

The four, two girls and two boys, apparently had the support of the silent majority of their classmates. The (four) went to the principal's office and announced they did not like the way the teacher was running things; they were unhappy about the homework; and they wanted a change.

The principal, a lady with years experience dealing with youngsters, was faced with a new type approach. She asked what the children planned to do if there was no change.

"Strike," was the one word ultimatum.

The principal announced she would check into the situation. A few minutes later she walked into the third grade and said she had reached her decision; things would be different for those unhappy with the third grade.

The protesting quartet beamed. Their silent supporters still said nothing. Then the principal announced, "Everyone who does not like the third grade may come with me—to the second grade."

The protesting quartet was stunned. The silent majority was just that, silent. Class resumed.

What a magnificent example of the reason so many students are rattled by the time they graduate from high school! Why on earth are kids being given homework in the *third grade?* What has happened to the idea of *childhood?* Why didn't the teacher *talk* with the kids, instead of immediately responding with, "And what if I don't?" Yeah, the class resumed—and I'll bet that those kids will never forget the response of that principal and that teacher. "Love it or leave it, kids." Just like Nixon. Just like Beulah. Just like Agnew. Just like all of us "wise" adults. Just like the disciples:

> They brought young children to Christ, that he should touch them: and his disciples rebuked those that brought them. But when Jesus saw it, he was much displeased, and said unto them, "Suffer the little children to come unto me, and forbid them not: for of such is the kingdom of God. Verily I say unto you, Whosoever shall not receive the kingdom of God as a little child, he shall not enter therein." And he took them up in his arms, put his hands upon them, and blessed them.

May 18

One year ago today, I gave my last sermon in the Jersey parish. It was such a weird event, so many conflicting emotions, too many uncertainties, too few explanations of what had happened.

The parishioners held the weekly bulletin which briefly and

politely announced that I had been asked to leave. Those hundreds of familiar faces carried such differing and odd expressions: some kindness here, certain hate there, a majority of confusion everywhere.

The sermon was a schizoid combination of hopeful dignity and pathetic beggings for a chance to stay in town to do a "street ministry."

I've rewritten those words a hundred times in my mind, and my fantasies ache for a second chance to climb into that elevated pulpit, to be *un*dignified and *ir*rational and *un*begging, to scream some heroic statement into those congregated faces, to vent the immobilizing anger in my gut, to demand some specific charges against me which could be denied or defended or debunked. But fantasies are fantasies only.

One year ago today, and I have yet to recover from the divorce of it all. I have yet to understand what inconsistency or inefficiency could have demanded such a quick and conclusive ending to a seemingly auspicious beginning.

Were my sermons too "dovish?" Were my liturgies too outrageous? Were my questions too contagious? Were my pastoral calls too infrequent? Were my ideals too divisive? Were my hopes too grandiose? Or was I finally—totally—unacceptable in these and all of the other ways?

One year ago today I told myself that I would find some stability, some certainty, some tenure in this vocation. And here I am asking myself the same questions, but in a different job in a different place at a different time.

It seems like ten years.

May 19

The U.C.M. Board had its monthly meeting last night, and the general tension of this city was obvious in our own group. There was a subdued acceptance of the staff efforts in the past two weeks, but I think that there were some unvoiced feelings of anger or uncertainty or something.

The Board decided to hire Mike Kulczycki as the "intern" on next year's staff, and that prospect delights me. That makes three of us for next year, but we still have no replacement for Tom Niccolls. I've gone through about thirty dossiers so far, with no real candidates apparent. I hope someone shows up soon—I'm starting to sweat.

Logan's, the main bookstore, placed a large ad in today's paper: "It becomes increasingly important that as our community returns to some degree of normalcy we do not forget the tremendous job done by the Athens Police Force. With such an irrational and irresponsible element trying to provoke a violent incident, the Athens Police Force maintained its cool . . ."

May 23

The following anonymous letter arrived at the house today:

> If we had a few more *quack* preachers in Athens, all our *troubles* would disappear. I hear one is leaving and good riddance. Another may go if he is *rode out on a rail*. I'm not a *Presby* but know about what they had to endure and have heard from different ones that you were a *second Lieu* (Lew). Some *compliment* I would say. There is nothing quite so *despiseable* as a *wolf in sheeps clothing* and the only reason they are *anti war* is they are *yellow* to the bone and too *lazy* to work.

Ahh, the joys of receiving a billet-doux from a secret admirer! No, I can't joke about it, for it pretty much ruined my day. I keep telling myself that I'm not going to read anonymous letters when they arrive but, of course, I read them anyway.

One of the men this cretin was referring to is Lew Kemmerle, a Presbyterian minister who was pastor of the local church in Athens, one of the two "in" churches in town. Lew made the age-old mistake of attempting to preach the Christian Gospel in a Christian church, and so he is hated by many of the upstanding citizens of this town. Lew participated in the march in Selma (one of the ultimate sins of the sixties), talked about the Black Panthers, preached against the war, and did most of the other things which his conscience, not his core congregation, demanded. He was then put through the obscenity of an "open forum" on his behavior and ministry, and, of course, he was finally faced with resigning his position. I've seen a number of guys canned from jobs in the church; but rarely have I seen one eliminated with such inhumanity as was done here.

I often think that there are two things which a parish does better than anything else: build a new building and fire the pastor. If the energies in those two situations were channeled into the numerous problems in this country, we would surely inaugurate the age of hope and prosperity for all. But it's more fun to build the building or fire the pastor.

Anyway, I *do* consider it a compliment to be compared with Lew, although I'm not too wild about the trip out of town on the rail! I wonder if the letter writer would say anything to me face-to-face. I've gotta quit reading those things.

May 28

We try futilely, I know, to "explain ourselves" to the angry community via a newsletter:

> ***We initiated a three-day *fast* of clergy, students and faculty to express our anguish at killing in Asia and at Kent State—and to present alternative life-styles. Communion was served on the College Green at noon.
> ***The fifty fasters served as a disciplined corps of marshalls

for a silent March against Murder which saw 2,500 people participate. We *rejected* radical demands for a sit-in on the state highway.

***We addressed rallies and talked to *hundreds* of students urging peaceful and lawful means of dissent.

***We helped organize workshops and seminars on the College Green and provided office facilities for students committed to keeping the University *open.* Little of this was reported in the news media.

***We organized a telegram of protest to President Nixon, which was sent with 3,000 signatures.

***We sent a letter at the end of the first eight days commending the police for their restraint and discipline under extreme conditions. We saw that suspended students left town.

***We remained in constant communication with the administration to give our interpretation of student feeling.

***We provided lodging for 60 coeds when tear gas drove them out of their dormitory.

***We provided counsel for parents of students who were arrested during the disturbance.

There are probably other things which we could have done to keep the University open—but we couldn't think of them then or now.

It's a "kissy" document, one I'm not terribly proud of, one that won't change anyone's mind, but the hostility is pervasive —and we *do* want to continue to exist here!

May 29

A fellow named Fred Mong has been here the last two days to interview for the Niccolls' position. He has been a campus pastor in South Dakota for a few years, and he shows the battle scars. I assume that he has somewhat the same reputation we do, and he seems anxious to find a new spot. The discussions have been good—and *animated*—and I feel quite attracted to him as a coworker. Paranoia from New Jersey flashes by. What if I make a mistake, and things don't work.

Niccolls—on whom I depend so much for judgment and support—is not taking a very active role in this search, for he doesn't want to force his own "bias." I wish he would, for I seem to trust his biases more than my own.

I'm going to recommend that we hire Mong.

June 1

A letter came by special delivery today. It was from a female student whom I have been counseling during the past year on a few occasions. She is not terribly unusual in her viewpoint, demeanor, appearance. Unfortunately, she is also not unusual in her relationship with her parents, for I have experienced too many cases of similar situations. Her letter reads as follows:

Sun. Nite. 11:30 pm

Tom—

I've put off writing this letter and asking for help as long as I can—any longer and I can guarantee myself cracking up.

(For about the billionth time) tonight I've lain in bed listening to my "Mother & Father" talk about me—what a degenerate, lousy, ungrateful (they're right there) worthless daughter & person I am. Everyday my "Mother" has to tell me how I irritate her (when I'm not even doing anything) & how I'll never amount to anything etc. etc. My nerves just can't take this anymore—I'm not allowed to use the car or go anywhere or do anything—the dog's feelings are cared for more than mine.

Even when S. was here last year she couldn't believe it. I thought after that letter I wrote things might get better, but they play nicey nicey for a few minutes until I get home & the same old shit starts again.

I'm tired of crying myself to sleep every night.

I'm tired of feeling like an intruder in this house.

I'm tired of being kicked in the teeth for nothing & I can't take anymore. My brother will be home next Monday for 3 weeks &

things shouldn't be too bad then but after he leaves it'll just be worse.

I know they're not letting me go back to school even though they won't admit it to me & I was going to try to stay here all summer & work & send myself back in the fall but I don't think I can make it for 3 more months without cracking.

If I leave here do you think you could help me find a cheap place to live & a full time job in Athens. I don't have a car so it would have to be close in. It's either that or VISTA.

Please, Tom, I really feel like I'm losing grip on everything anymore. I'm tired of talking to myself all the time to keep from screaming & throwing things. I do it all the time—out loud.—sometimes even at work.

I guess its hit me that I can't do it by myself.

Maybe VISTA is the answer—for a while anyway.

This is the 4th letter I've written—the others have been torn up because I thought I'd at least *try* the summer—but I really really don't think I can anymore. If you write back please address it S. I. as my mother takes every opportunity (S. is her first name too) to open my mail & she's quite used to saying she didn't look closely at the envelope etc. Please answer me, Tom.

I know that I don't have the right to impose myself & my problems on you or anyone for that matter—but I really know you're the only one I could go to.

S. in Hell

This girl is certainly not "innocent" in all of this trouble with her family, and her parents must accept the responsibility for what *they* are doing. The sad part of it all is that they are simply destroying each other in a geometric progression of frustration, broken hopes, and categorical expectations.

What is it that we expect of each other in the family? What exactly do we want our kids or our spouse to *do* or *be*? Maybe it would help us all to stop for awhile, make out a list of expectations for each person in the family, and then review the list, item by item, with the continuing question of: WHY? Maybe all of us could read R. D. Laing's books (*Knots* and *The Politics of the Family*), but we probably won't. Instead, perhaps we will discuss the world problems or our problems at work or the new property taxes or something else which rightly grabs our interest; it is, though, at the expense of the dynamics which may be going on under our very noses in the living room and kitchen. Do I—do you—know who lives in this house, and why?

I must do something with this girl. As with all the rest I have seen, I will listen; I will listen while she attempts to grope through the anger and the confusion of breaking away. I don't think it always has to be so.

June 2

At the Board meeting last night, it was agreed to make an offer to Fred Mong to be co-director, starting in August. I'm relieved—and somewhat hesitant.

Don Craig is going off the staff here this summer, so that he can devote himself totally to his doctoral work. So now I lose two of the finest men I could ever hope to work with. I regret it deeply, but I suppose that we must simply celebrate the time we had together.

Oh, how I hate the demands and pace of this world—no one is in one place for very long—or perhaps I have just encountered that myself. But it seems that everyone is constantly *moving*—in and out, up and down, hello and good-bye, write when you can, send a recent picture, when are we going to see you again, how are the kids, hug each other for me, you mean so much to us. . . . Then why do we part?

June 9

Something that continues to haunt me is the memory of a universitywide faculty meeting which Tom and I attended recently. If there was ever a thought in my mind that the faculty was "liberal," that event ended it.

Unbelievable. Faculty members attempting to speak against the war were shouted down by angry mouths which spit in hate. Sowle tried to maintain some sanity, but it was a mob scene, and I left after forty minutes. I only wish that it had been filmed so that the absent students could see their "responsible elders" at work.

It's going to be a bitter year.

June 11

At 9:45 this morning, I received a brief, anonymous phone call. The message was clear: "I'm goin' to blow your goddamn head off, preacher!"

I got the message.

I shook for an hour.

Why in hell did he say *that?*

Better not tell Jude.

June 13

God I love to do weddings! They seem to be the one part of the ministry job which consistently makes me happy. I love the premarital discussions, the planning, the honest conversations, the celebration, the affection, the joy.

So few of the weddings are "straight" anymore. At least the ones I am asked to do. I don't think I have done a "Prayer Book wedding" all year. I suppose that makes me a heathen, but I don't think the bishop would be too upset—he seems to enjoy humanity.

The kids nowadays are trying to get away from the "shift of property" aspect of weddings, away from the bride as a hunk of property which is passed from father to son-in-law. Rather, we are often giving *both* the bride and the groom "away," as a symbolic act at the beginning of the service, so that I can "give them back" to the assembled community at the end.

Weddings seem to me to be one of the few occasions left in our society when people can say lovely, embarrassing things to each other in public. I *want* the service to be embarrassing, to reflect all of the crazy things which human beings can *feel* about each other. Of course it's schmaltzy—but in a world which celebrates violence and death, why shouldn't we have great observances of love and romance and community concern?

So the kids are writing their own vows, saying what *they* want to say, knowing that a vow is a very existential thing, a "promise" which is made in the present, with a hope for the future. You can't promise about your feelings in twenty years, but you can verbally hope to grow and understand.

I know that it might shock the little old fellow in the back pew, but I find it encouraging that young people are living together for awhile before marriage nowadays. I don't really see much of an alternative. The divorce rate is skyrocketing, and there are simply too many aspects of personality which must be understood before people can make a lifelong contract. Of course, a method of birth control is a necessity in this arrangement, so that a child does not result from the experiment in living.

Anyway, it is a joy for me to be in the midst of these public declarations of commitment, and I find it difficult to ever accept a "fee" for officiating. The event itself is a reward to my spirits.

We leave for a two-week vacation in Canada tomorrow.

HALLELUJAH!

July 4

We return from the nonpolitical, restful, sunny shores of Lake Huron in Ontario—where we played in the sand and the water, where we spent hours in joyful conversation with visiting friends—and we are back to the same tension and animosity which saturated the town before we left.

Canada is so damned misleading. While there, I could only think that it wasn't as "sick" as the U.S., that somehow the people were "better" or "more understanding" or something —but that's too easy. If Canada were in the same mess we are, I know that the people would respond in the same ways to each other: fear, hesitation, superpatriotism, conspiracy paranoia, and all the rest. But maybe the Canadians can learn some things from us before they get too far along the road to domestic despair.

From whom do *we* learn?

July 11

A "Committee on Campus Disorders" from the state legislature has been in town for the past couple of days, collecting testimony and ostensibly trying to understand the campus situation. What a joke. I think that the Committee was a real help to the situation here, though, for the members were so utterly obnoxious to everyone that they provided the same frustration which the students have been experiencing all along. Even the "straight" townspeople who testified were treated with disdain and contempt, and the *Messenger* reported it as such.

In the middle of my own testimony—as I tried to explain the local effect of a disastrous national policy decision—

Senator Cook (Toledo) blurted out to those sitting next to him, "Who is this guy!" Later, when Cook was listening to the acting student-council president—a very straight-looking young man—he couldn't believe that the student was sympathetic with the antiwar feelings of May. "Here we have a fine looking, all-American young man," Cook said, "and I'm very disappointed to hear this sort of testimony come from him!" Cook later added that the legislature will have to take the power into its own hands. It probably will . . .

July 14

At the Board meeting last night, most of the discussion centered on the subject of improving U.C.M.'s "image." Good grief, we're desperate!

July 23

It was three years ago, but it remains branded on my brain as if it were this morning. That instant of terror will never be forgotten.

Judy and I had gone to bed realizing that something serious was happening in Detroit—on the other side of town from our parish—but we could get no information on the radio.

At two A.M., I awoke because of the ringing of our phone in the next room—I stumbled through the dark, finally knocking the phone off the shelf, grabbing for the receiver. A blank dial tone drilled my ear. As I groped my way back to bed, a bit upset by the "prank call," I decided for some unknown reason to take a look out of the window, which was totally covered by a shade.

I lifted the shade quickly, took a glimpse of the neighborhood, and realized that I wasn't breathing. Before me leaped huge, orange flames from the next street—I looked in both directions, only to see more flames.

My God, what is happening! What do I do!

Judy was still asleep, and Jenny, eight months old, was in a room down the hall. A million thoughts pass through my mind.

Will we be killed?

Will the flames spread to this street?

Where are the sirens—there should be sirens!

What will I do if someone attacks the house?

I couldn't move for about three minutes—I stood at the window and watched the flames. Suddenly, I didn't want to be alone.

"Jude . . . Jude, wake up—now I don't want you to get too excited, but I think the whole city is on fire."

"Okay, I won't get excited."

She was out of bed as she said the words, and the two of us huddled on the floor, alternately looking out the window and watching the tiny Sony television screen. The speaker informed us that we were in the midst of a citywide rebellion, that National Guard troops were on duty, that federal troops were probably going to arrive shortly.

What little I knew of black history in this country flashed back and forth through my mind incessantly, and I reached the conclusion that I was probably deserving of death—but I sure didn't want to die!

I learned more about myself and my world in that week than I had in seven years of college. If it was, in fact, a "racial" uprising, then it was not apparent to me, for we were not harmed, yelled at, or spurned by the black population. The only time I was hassled was an occasion when a white cop insulted me for absolutely no reason. I really don't know why. I saw the police do some terrible things that week, and I became prejudiced because of it. Judy pointed out that the police were simply occupation troops who had been given a free hand by the officials of Detroit—she mentioned that they were as scared as the rest of the population. Yes, scared and tired and uptight and human. But I can't forgive some of the things I saw. They happened, and I cannot erase them from my memory. Surely, too, many of the police have their own memories of horror and waste. No one won; everyone lost.

I had lunch at the drugstore behind the church toward the end of the week—I was the only white person inside the place except for the owner—a girl had a dog with her, and as she went out the door, she looked at the dog and said, "Come on, whitefolks." Everyone turned and looked at me—I got the message, but I realized that some of those people were embarrassed by the incident. Others weren't.

The same day, I met a black photographer who told me that the two major wire services had employed him that week to take pictures for them in the ghetto. He added that those same wire services had never been interested in his work previously. "But I'm black and they're white, and they're scared and I'm still black. They want some pictures of the blacks rioting, but they won't accept the *real* pictures."

He opened his valise and showed me the picture of a nine-year-old girl who had been shot through the head—there was a huge hole in her right temple. He said that the National Guard had done that, but no one in suburbia would believe it. "Fuck it," he said, as he zipped the valise.

On one sidewalk, I saw a group of about twenty black people and one white fellow, most of them crying. He was one of the few white *or* black merchants who didn't try to screw the local population with exorbitant prices—and people were mourning the loss of his store, for he didn't have the cash to rebuild.

The black residents of our block had received nightly phone calls telling them to paint "soul power" on their houses so that they wouldn't be burned. Our neighbors didn't give in to that anonymous demand, and several of the black women stayed with Judy and Jenny when I was out on the streets at night.

We received more love than we deserved.

On the following Saturday, the word got around the area that some "help" was arriving from the suburbs—that a truck was bringing in food and blankets for the people who had been burned out. I was elated. I waited on the street with a crowd of about three hundred people, waiting for the huge semi-trailer which finally arrived. Amidst the obvious anticipation, the rear doors were opened. Instead of food and blankets, out spilled hundreds of used and broken appliances —toasters, irons, fry pans—everything you could imagine which had been used for several years and then thrown out . . .

At first, I thought that it was the cruelest of jokes.

As the crowd walked away in silence, though, I knew that it was simply a symbol of the total lack of communication and understanding which exists now in our cities.

July 25

It has been an odd month. Rather than experiencing the traditional summer of a lighter caseload—of sending God on summer vacation as we normally do in the church—I find the consistent demands of pregnancies, draft problems, divorce situations, and all the rest.

This past week I was confronted by two very gentle people who wanted to get married. Two problems; both are slightly under twenty-one, and they are of different races. I told them that I couldn't marry them because of the age situation, but I suggested that they go to Kentucky. Consequently, I looked for a priest's name in the national clergy directory, and directed them to him. Yesterday I received a call from him. He introduced himself, asked me my opinion on the stability of the relationship, and finally assured me that everything was fine. I found out today that when the couple arrived at his church, he sent his *wife* over to see them, to tell them that he couldn't do the ceremony! No real reason stated, except that the local bishop thought it "best" not to get involved. I want to vomit. The couple then went to a female justice of the peace, and they were treated with dignity. I'm beginning to think that the last place to look for the true church is in the church.

My anxiety was lessened by a magnificent and warm wedding this morning in the campus chapel. Eric Roth—who had spent so much time with me during the May activities—was married to Karol Bailey, a sensitive and loving woman. Eric's father apologized to me for his tears during the service—little did he realize how much I celebrate such open expression— and how often I regret the stony faces at such occasions. It was nice.

July 31

A great feast of joy and tears at our house tonight for the going-away party for the Niccolls family. I know of no way to express my feelings about it. We gave him a large-framed print of Rouault's *Clown* but it was only a tiny symbol of the great love which we all have for him . . .

Joe Polak is gone too. I embraced him in early May when he made his announcement, and he goes now to be the campus rabbi at Boston University. How much he has grown in understanding—and how much I will miss his empathy.

And Don Craig is gone too.

And now we try to form a whole new relationship on the staff.

August 4

A young guy came to see me for counseling, and I realized very quickly that he is an obsessive compulsive, if such a label is of any help. Well, at least it helps me to realize that his situation is way beyond my competency. He is obsessed with the number *three* and with the word (or idea) of *Tuesday*. Whenever he sees three of anything, he becomes rather immobilized. On Tuesdays, he becomes lethargic or frightened or both. He has been suicidal, and I knew that it had been a great effort for him to reach out for help. A lovable guy, really, but I didn't feel adequate for the task of therapy, so I arranged an appointment for him with my friend Earl, the university psychiatrist.

Earl presents one of the ironies of life: I have deep respect for him, and greatly enjoy his company, but we rarely get together; somehow we both are too busy, and our contacts are mostly on a professional level. I wonder why I let that happen —or not happen, whichever it is.

I have been invited to speak at the Presbyterian Church on Sunday, and I feel as though I'm really on the spot to make some sort of explanation of U.C.M. to a congregation which has been quite antagonistic in the past. Not all of them, but some.

August 9

Today was the day for the sermon at the Presbyterian Church, an event which carried great ambivalence in my gut. The whole thing seemed like an immense ritual, not unlike a bullfight! Careful preparation of both syntax and vestment, the summing up of courage, the quick look in the mirror to make sure that the garments are in proper array—and, then, picking up the beat of some Gothic hymn, I burst into the arena to face the crowd.

The adults grab surreptitious glimpses of me as they pick their way through the dated hymn; the children mouth the same words, but somehow know that the whole setting is a bit absurd and confusing and boring, and so they quietly touch and smile at each other. I have decided to "lay it on the line" in the sermon, which means, in homiletical terms, that I want to be at least half-truthful about the gospel; to be 10-percent truthful means to end up with the normal, ghastly sermon which evokes the usual, enthusiastic "good sermon" remarks at the door; to be 80-percent truthful means to court disaster. For better or worse, these are some excerpts of what I had to say:

> I must listen to my soul for the whisper that is there, and then I must shout out to you. But what will happen if I pour out my soul and change that whisper to a shout?
>
> . . . My friends, the question is not: What *would* Christ do in this place, in this town, in this country, in this world. The question is: What *is* Christ doing in these places, in peoples' lives; what *is* he saying in a whisper in your soul and mine . . . ?
>
> You and I both know that I have been called a communist by some, and a pig by others, and I'm sure that other rather descriptive terms will be developed this year, not only for me, but also for the new staff members . . .
>
> We have tried to listen and look for the direction which the Christ would have us take in this world. That is always risky business . . .
>
> Sometimes, like you, we listen with honesty, and sometimes, like you, we do less than that. But when we listen with honesty, we are called to *act* in that same integrity . . .
>
> Jesus Christ keeps saying: ACCEPT, ACCEPT, LISTEN, LISTEN MORE, REACH OUT, MINISTER; and at the very same moment, the morés or etiquette or laws of our society may be saying: REJECT, TURN AWAY, REJECT, DENY, IGNORE, REJECT. *That is the tension,* and that is where the name-calling begins . . .

We cannot equate Jesus Christ with the United States of America. We cannot equate Jesus Christ with any President or Congress or mayor or city or economic system or political system—and certainly we cannot equate Him with any campus minister!

It would, of course, be very pleasant if every person in my ministry was perfect, educated, clean, totally organized, and in agreement with me on everything, but they are as varied as we are. Many of the people whom I see everyday have absolutely no use for the Church, for the Church has had no use for them . . . I will not apologize for our ministry to all of them, whether repugnant or attractive. And you—you must not refrain from *your* ministry either . . .

I do not know of one instance when any member of the U.C.M. staff has ever advocated violence to anyone, and yet I hear the same rumors that you do—but the rumors never seem to have any *specific* details to them . . . I have come to the conclusion that such rumors are started by people who *want* to see violence—and I wonder what whispers they are hearing in *their* souls . . .

I happen to believe that we can build a future together, if we will allow each other to live and minister as we must. You do not *have* to like me, and you do not *have* to agree with me—you only have to listen to the demanding, hoping whispers in your own soul . . .

The handshakes and comments during the social hour suggested that I had come pretty close to the 50-percent truthful mark.

August 15

A year ago today we arrived here. Whew.

On the Church calendar, this is the feast day of the "Assumption of the Virgin Mary," a doctrine which was important at some time in the Church's history but is an anachronism now. But it still exists—and no one really knows why. A friend tells me that they had a unique way of celebrating the occasion out at Stanford: a group of people would form a circle with a young coed named Mary in the center—and everyone would assume that she was a virgin. It seems like a rather interesting comment on some of the crazy things the Church tries to pass off on people.

August 18

Tom Niccolls' warm letter regarding my sermon of last week arrived. It concluded:

> I am still not positive about what a chaplain should do in this day and age, but I keep reminding myself that it is more important what he is and will try to let the doing follow. The clown always is tempted to alleviate the anxiety of his marginality, to move into a functionality and usefulness defined by the society he is marginal to, but if he does he loses his freedom and his ability to shape a new world or believe that one is being made anew. This matter of trust ain't the easiest thing in the world, is it?
>
> love,
> Tom

I doubt that Tom will ever really admit to himself that he possesses the depths of love and understanding and perception which are found in too few people. And he will probably never see in himself that understanding of the "chaplaincy" which is so utterly obvious to all of those who are around him. Maybe it is best that Tom never truly understand the basic beauty of his life. But I often wish he could.

The staff is starting to meet—we are feeling each other out, trying to establish ties, trying to ascertain biases, trying to build enough trust to communicate honestly. It is such a weird process, this thing we humans do with each other, just trying to express our understandings of life. I heard from a psychiatrist in New York that people send *thousands* of non-verbal messages to each other in the course of a normal conversation—messages about status, sex, goals, fears, and all the things we want to say but don't say verbally. There must be a *million* signals dashing around the room in our staff meetings.

August 31

A bombshell in the mail today at U.C.M.: the September issue of *Renewal* magazine, including four major articles on campus ministry. The first—and the one to stagger me as few things have in the past five years—is entitled "Campus Ministry: An Epitaph," by John Ferrell, a fraction of which follows:

> Forget it, fellows. Tomorrow morning at 9:00 A.M. all campus ministers should resign. There is no continuing rationale for the profession.
> Campus ministry doesn't exist anyway. It's gone.
> Gone with college fraternities, panty raids, and the civil rights movement. . . . The effort to tie into the student "movement" of the 1960's has gone the way of the movement itself: into oblivion.
> We tried to keep it alive: UCM organizing, civil rights and anti-war activism, ecumenicism, ecologism, etc. Always *following* public events, rather than charting our own autonomous path, we have run out of movements and issues to co-opt for the Church's ministry in higher education . . .
> Ministering to "The University" seemed a more sophisticated, more professional task than the "student work" ministries which preceded in the 1960's. . . . We were on the bandwagon.
> What was called "presence ministry" was a cop-out for those who could not otherwise discover a meaningful role as university ministers. It was dramatic, exciting, and ego building—but it was a non-functional style for a non-existent profession.
> The truth is, of course, we *were* doing vitally important things: those things determined by *other people* to be important, and which they were doing anyway with or without our leadership . . .
> It's clear now that all the movement failures of the 1960's have

bred a new generation of cynical, bitter college students. They developed a deep distrust for *all* institutions, including the Church and its expression on the campus. . . . The Revolution left the white middle class—and the Church's campus ministry . . .

It is clear that the Church's ministry to the University must face up to its own bankruptcy. . . . Campus clergy have had it—even the best of them—*especially* the best of them. The Church's ministry can take place only in a parish-community setting—a community of self-conscious Christians . . .

There is really only one principal task to be performed by clergymen: the priestly and pastoral ministry (there just aren't many prophets around). . . . Seminary graduates in time become pretty good counselors, fair preachers, excellent B.S. artists, and that's about as far as it goes in terms of practical skills.

Those campus ministers who want to continue to function as the Church's clergymen should return to the parish, where they would regain their integrity and perform clear professional duties: propogating the Gospel, gathering the Church, and visiting the sick. Those men who want to spend their time doing other things should stop the masquerade and work for a different paymaster . . .

The other three articles try courageously to answer Ferrell, but the result is wanting in conviction. I don't really know what to do with this—to ignore it, to argue vainly against it, to share it with the new staff, or to simply agree with it, and resign tomorrow.

The article is accurate, but I don't have the energy, the courage, or even the inclination to hang it all up tomorrow morning at nine. I shall "judiciously consider" it, as my more conservative brothers would say. Which means I'm confused . . . and a bit scared.

VI

"During the New York days, people told me Eliot was writing the same message in men's rooms all over town."
"Do you remember what it was?"
"Yes. **'If you would be unloved and forgotten, be reasonable.'** "

—Kurt Vonnegut, Jr.,
God Bless You, Mr. Rosewater

September 11, 1970

After twenty-five hours of pain, struggling, and several unholy epithets, Judy finally gave birth to our daughter this morning! Lisa Elizabeth Jackson. All red and wrinkled and aggravated with the sudden abrasiveness of this outside world. And gorgeous. I would like to write something eloquent about my joy and relief and pride on this day, but I am not eloquent. On the way home from the hospital, I wept, just as I did when we received Jenny and Peter. Anyway, Jude knows my love for her—and that is enough for me.

During the long hours of waiting in the "father's room," I reflected a little on abortion. My mind hasn't changed. I cannot use my present joy as a universal balm for the ubiquitous despair of scorned and tortured children.

In an ideal world, of course, we could all be against abortion because there wouldn't be any need for it.

In an ideal world, perhaps we would provide birth-control

methods openly, without the attendant guilt and Victorian shame and secrecy.

In an ideal world, perhaps we would take care of children, without labeling them as "bastards" and passing them from foster home to foster home each month—we wouldn't ignore adoptive children because they happen to have red hair or different skin tones or physical handicaps.

In an ideal world we would not have the constant barrage of sex-oriented advertisements which incessantly tell people that to be accepted they must impersonally "put out."

In an ideal world the church could take the sexual activities of life out of the ambiguity of the Garden of Eden into the concreteness of everyday life.

But the original meaning of utopia is "no place."

We must make decisions in the midst of imperfection and be ready to change if we are wrong.

Today, though, the world *does* seem ideal with Lisa's first, crying breath.

September 14

Everyone is uptight about the possible mood of the returning students, and no one seems to know what it might be.

After the closing last spring, several of the more militant students were banned from Athens County for two years by Judge Sheeter—it was a convenient way of attempting to quiet things down. But the real question mark now lies with the entering freshmen. They represent an entirely new population, one which may reflect the anger of last year—or one which may instill a very different atmosphere to these halls. I wonder.

September 21

Here in the university—a place ostensibly dedicated to learning—it is the administrators who are the important figures, not the faculty or students. It is the administrator who is constantly in the newspaper or on the radio, rendering new decisions, edicts, or policies which will affect the lives of thousands of people. The faculty is really very rarely heard from—they go to their classes and/or do their research. But anytime a new issue arises, it is some administrator, some "expert in human relations parameters," who renders the ultimate answer. And the administrators are joined by the trustees —a group of people who live hundreds of miles away, who rarely visit the campus or town, who never actually experience the particulars of dormitory or classroom life—and they "help" make the decisions!

There is something very wrong with the whole arrangement. We administrators are overwhelming people. We have too many committees dealing with too many lives, not our own. We control every building, every policy, every life.

Who are we, and how did we get to this point of omni-control?

We *are* Pharisees!

September 22

We have had several staff meetings in the past few weeks, and the various relationships are forming in different ways. I have a strong attraction to Don—he tries to be open, he is somewhat new to this vocation, and he is not as skeptical as I feel.

Mike, of course, has been a good friend in the past, works

hard at listening, writes his thoughts on paper surreptitiously during staff meetings, and allows us to vent our thoughts.

Fred is a strong personality, still weary from the constant battles in his last job, full of anger about the treatment he has received from the Church in the past. I must admit that we are not terribly comfortable with each other as yet, for we both display a similar aggressiveness, and—somehow—we seem to compete with each other. I haven't figured it out yet.

In one lengthy session, I attempted to explain my financial situation, for I am concerned that it could become a matter of resentment among us. My father left a rather large estate, and my family is most benevolent—so I receive income beyond my salary, income which allows Judy and me to do things and go places. I received a lot of flak in my seminary days because of this issue, and yet I still find myself somehow apologizing for our situation. I shouldn't, but I do. The issue affects the staff, for a sizeable portion of the funding campaign was pledged from my family, and I don't want any staff member to think that we are hoping to "control" U.C.M. because of that. But it allows me to control my own life a bit better.

Let's face it—I was speaking mainly to Fred. He has told me about the severe financial limitations which he experienced during seminary—how he had to forgo law school because of a lack of funds, how he would love to combine his present experience with a law degree, but there is seemingly no way to afford that schooling now. Absurdly, I feel guilty about that.

All of us realize the increasing deadness in the church: the constant loss of money and members, the reaction to campus unrest, the retreat into the sanctuary in so many places. We have talked for hours on the devastating article on campus ministry in *Renewal*. We have tried to imagine what we will do when the church simply has no more money or jobs for campus ministers. We just keep talking about it all, and we get nowhere, except a bit more depressed with each discussion.

I'm beginning to think that we are too much alike—too

many of the same opinions and feelings and frustrations. Maybe we need to quickly hire a "staff optimist" to counter all of our skepticism with happy thoughts. No, Fred and I would probably beat him up.

So, what now? I'm excited as hell about the possibility of starting a "crisis center" here, to give people a place or a phone they can contact. A couple of grad students have been working on this idea for the past several months with little success, but I think we can do it with a big push and some cooperation from the university. Onward and upward!

September 23

Boy, we wounded the ecumenical movement today!

The Campus Ministry Association had decided a couple of weeks ago to have a day-long session today, so that all of us could get to know each other better, express our feelings, and state our goals. We on the staff, however, decided that we needed some time right now to get our act together, and so we announced at the beginning of the session that we had to leave at lunchtime, rather than at five.

Explosion! The hostility came from every direction, and it was aimed mainly at me, I suppose because I was the only veteran from U.C.M.

"Do you realize that you've ruined the entire session with your casual announcement?"

"We didn't mean to ruin anything," I countered. "It's just that a lot of things have suddenly come up among the staff, and we feel that we must do some immediate planning."

"It seems as though you could have notified us!"

"We *are* notifying you! Oh come on now, we've got a few hours to talk, so let's get at the agenda." I knew that the agenda had changed.

"Well I'm pissed off," another member shouted. "You guys

seem to think that you *are* the campus ministry around here. Hell, even your 'United Campus Ministry' name implies it!"

I was angry. "Look," I said, "you know damned well that the name is national, not local. If you're uptight about the name, then let's all merge into one body, have one staff, one budget, one program, and all the rest." As appealing as that sounded to me, I knew that the odds on a merger of Protestant, Catholic, and Jewish ministries were six zillion to one.

"Tell me something, Jackson," another demanded, "how is it that you always manage to get your picture on the front page of the *Post*?"

At last we get to the nitty-gritty. "Oh for God's sake, do we have to get into that sort of stuff! I'm not going to apologize if the *Post* staff happens to think that we're doing worthwhile things. If it's that important to you, then go do something that will satisfy the picture editor!"

The entire morning was filled with such mutual, imbecilic dialogue, and we certainly got to know each other better! Fred tried to quiet things a bit, but not much success.

We were unfair in our initial announcement. Yet, I am amazed at the *sort* of anger which existed. Finally, of course, we all sounded like a group of insurance salesmen, haggling over the commission on our "heavenly policies." And I know that the haggling isn't going to stop here.

September 24

The students are back in town, back in classes. A lot of tension and uncertainty in the air, although things are extremely quiet. Some new, tough legislation hangs over everyone's head regarding campus unrest, and that fact pervades most conversations.

September 26

We just finished a two-day conference of the Board and staff—and it was disastrous! Everyone involved is either slightly or massively depressed.

Laten Carter, our "state-level man," laid it on us about a possible large cut in income from the national churches. In fact, we are receiving a *partial* payment *this month*.

Laten, in his natural gentleness and affection, tried to bolster the spirits, but it didn't work. Even the farm setting of the conference didn't help. The facts—or our perception of the facts—spoke for themselves.

Last December, when the Board had such a great conference together, we did a corporate fantasy on what we would do with an additional hundred thousand dollars—just to see what sort of priorities we had. Now, we take most of the same people and tell them that we are losing our funding rapidly, that our priorities may go down the tubes. What do we expect besides depression?

October 1

There was a meeting in Baker Center to discuss the possibilities of getting this crisis center in gear.

I mentioned that the counseling case load at U.C.M. was heavier than I had ever seen it, and that we ought to cut all the normal red tape, if possible.

I was told, again, that I am entirely too impatient.

I am.

Why shouldn't I be?

October 8

U.C.M. offered an open showing of the new film *High School* tonight, and we had a huge crowd. There really isn't much one can say about the film, for its stark realism of the pathetic state of contemporary education is tragic in the extreme.

The school was an "average" one, and it seemed more like a prison than a center for learning. *Control* was obviously the key theme in the entire operation of the institution—keep the students quietly in a building all day, regardless of the methods which are needed to do so.

The film showed me why we receive so many myth-oriented questions in our "sexuality discussions" in the dorms: the high school athletic coach gave the "sex education" lecture to the males, and it was truly incredible! He was even more embarrassed and benighted than the young students . . .

Something has to be done. If we evade the improvement of the public school system, then we guarantee that the middle- and lower-class financial groups in our nation will continue to escape educational institutions at the earliest possible age, while those with the appropriate funds will increasingly opt for private education. That, of course, will finally spell financial bankruptcy for the public system.

Why can't we increase the amount of vocational training so that young people can learn trades—so many of the students here at O.U. do not belong in college—they don't want to be here—they want to participate in the practical skills of a certain craft—but they have been brainwashed into believing that they *must* go to college. I see this pressure especially in the upper-middle-class families—no one bothers to ask the kid what he really wants in life—there is an underlying embarrassment about a "well-off kid" wanting to be a plumber or an electrician or a carpenter or a mason or a mechanic. Not my son, we say.

October 9

The comments I wrote yesterday in regard to vocation were made personal today during a discussion with a student on my own life. The question was asked of me—as it has been asked a hundred times in the past: "Why are you a priest?"

My standard response has usually been: "That's the way I want to wake up every morning." That's true. To wake up with the knowledge that I am working another day in this vocation—well, it's enough to get me out of bed.

To be a priest is to be a generalist. It allows me to be a part of the lives of thousands of people—to speak with them, to listen to their hopes and tragedies, to embrace them. It allows me to be a public speaker, a private counselor, a celebrant of all sorts of public liturgies, a consultant, a motivater of groups, a planner, an administrator, or just about anything else I can get away with.

The collar I wear sometimes turns people off, for some individuals have had very negative experiences with a cold church or minister—but on the whole it serves the primary purpose of suggesting that I might be available to them for whatever reason. Ned Dougherty, my predecessor here, said that he wore the collar so that he wouldn't be mistaken for a freshman, and I suppose that there is some of that in my apparel too.

I don't think that I was "called" to the priesthood in any different manner than other men and women are "called" to their vocations. I have always seen that idea of a "religious call" as an overly developed bit of public relations on the part of the Church. Granted, some individuals experience an emotional catharsis, but I would hope that people would decide on the ministry with the same realism and honesty as they would use for any other decision. As I faced that decision myself, I tried to gauge the assets and liabilities which are a part of my character, the items in my personality which might help me or hinder me in doing the various "churchy" things that I described previously. I am the product of certain learnings which were given me by others, and it was those effects on my personality which led me to that decision.

To say that we clergymen suddenly turn miraculously from Saul to Paul is a hunk of wishful thinking. The men I knew in seminary were the products of immensely varied backgrounds, and I can think of few who had any sort of cathartic, religious experience to propel them into the ministry. Ordination, then, is a commitment to people, to the children of God, and that commitment is made with the same resolve, hesitation, and finiteness as is the commitment to any other vocation.

"Blessed" means to be made joyfully aware of one's life as a child of God. If a man or woman feels that in a particular vocation—however "prestigious" or not—then that person is blessed. I have felt myself thusly blessed because of the positive feelings of my own person in this particular vocation— and that is why I feel this deep anxiety about the direction of the ministry at this point in history. Like Paul, we are perhaps being led back to tentmaking—but I don't know how to make tents . . .

October 13

A young couple came to see me today about the "collapse" of their marriage. She wants to work on it, to resolve the problems, to gain some learnings—he wants out. He mentioned that he simply doesn't love her anymore, that he sees no reason to continue living with her. No animosity involved, but a realization that they have little of interest in common. It was

obvious to me that he brought her here so that I would pro-
nounce some "official" deathblow to their legal and personal
relationship. I told him that I could do little if he was totally
uninterested, but that I would gladly refer them to another
counselor if they wished.

They left the office.

They have been married for eight months.

Perhaps they wouldn't be heading across the street toward
the lawyer's office if some minister somewhere had suggested
that they live together for awhile before getting married.

October 20

We held a training session for the crisis-center volunteers
this afternoon, and I can see that we have a lot more to do.
Naturally, most of the participants seemed rather nervous
about their personal roles in counseling others, and that seems
to be a good sign—we should be nervous about working with
other peoples' lives. It was some of the "sure" people who
bothered me—they seemed to think that they could solve anyone's life problems.

I think that if we screened the applicants well and devoted
about three weeks to intensive training, we could be in adequate operation within a month. But I was reminded again
today that the red tape is getting thicker—that no one really
wants to take the responsibility within the university of putting
his name on the line for this venture. Everyone is uptight about
paraprofessionals. I understand that to a point, but, my God,
when are we going to admit that there simply aren't enough
facilities within this community at present to handle the multitudes of daily problems which people are experiencing? How
"professional" does a person have to be to *listen* to another
human being, to empathize, to express support and honest
concern?

There seems to be little reason in continuing this training if we are only going to disappoint the volunteers with another bureaucratic failure.

October 21

University Day, when classes are canceled and special events are planned, was oriented around the ecology issue. I participated in another panel discussion, this one on the population crisis, and we had a large audience.

The scientists on the panel mentioned most of the facts which Paul Ehrlich presented in his *Population Bomb,* and I attempted to list some of the birth-control factors.

The crunch came when several black students and one black faculty member contested the priorities of ecology and race. The blacks insisted that the entire ecology debate in this nation is obviously a middle-class concern, one which allows us to once again ignore the brutal, continuing aspect of white racism. One fellow also mentioned the feeling which I had heard on several occasions in Detroit: that birth control can be a convenient method of genocide against the black population.

It was a tense discussion with charges and countercharges between scientists and blacks. It was good, though, in that I knew that most of the white students in the audience had not heard these black arguments before, and I think that some of the students were stunned.

I have very mixed feelings about the argument. As a member of the white middle class, I have learned the ways of racism well, so that I would not naturally think of the black point of view. They have been crapped on enough to suspect any white issue, to wonder when we are going to quit diverting our attention from the issue which has existed for four hundred years! Yet, I cannot eliminate or ignore my concern over the population and pollution problems. I wonder which issue *does* have a higher priority in my own life . . .

October 23

Mike and I were invited out to a high school in a nearby town this morning to speak to a class of students which is attempting to get at some of the issues in our society. The presence of my collar caused many looks and much murmuring among the students—and as Mike and I walked toward the car to depart, a group of about ten guys yelled in our direction that we were "peace creeps."

Middle Americans aren't all over thirty.

October 25

We are being absolutely overwhelmed with counseling cases at U.C.M. I can't believe it. The campus is unusually quiet politically—our fears were unfounded, I guess—but students seem to be in a depressing lethargy about their own lives.

The problem pregnancies seem endless, and we are seeing ten and fifteen women per day! Many of these cases are not the result of "college life," for the majority of women were obviously impregnated before they ever got back to campus this fall. I wonder if the mothers of America are going to be more uptight about birth-control pills or pregnant daughters.

My appointment calendar looks like a road map—every hour is taken with more and more people, and there are four or five waiting in the hallway most of the time.

I am very pleased with the job that Don Bubenzer is doing. Fred and I have been in this racket for a few years and may expect this sort of onslaught, but Don is new—and he's working like a seasoned veteran. I wonder, though, how long it will be before we are all burned out by the masses. I hear from friends that the Health Center and the Psych Center are also overwhelmed with clients.

Still no word of any progress with the crisis center.

November 5

The meeting for the "U.C.M. Associates" was held tonight, and we had a pretty good crowd on hand. Fred did most of the talking, trying to present a logical reason for these people to get involved seriously with our operation.

I felt uncomfortable during most of the presentation, not only because of this unexplained tension between Fred and me, but also because of my hesitation with the entire concept of the meeting. I get increasingly uptight with the possibility of more and more people directing our program here, of trying to peddle ourselves off as a "straight" organization. I just don't think that explanations of our work will ultimately make any difference to this academic and civic community.

Of course, I have no right to act this way. I am in a financial position to take some risks which might not be possible for others to take, and I know that the staff is acutely aware of that fact. That is certainly part of the tension that I feel. Fred is working his ass off to put this thing together, and I must not torpedo it with my own skepticism. But it's hard to swallow.

I'm feeling very down at this point. Yeah, I have great times with many dear friends, when we laugh and celebrate with zest, but I can't seem to affect the direction of U.C.M. or the community or even my own life very much. I feel that I am losing control somehow. I don't know who in the hell to talk with about it, for the rest of the staff members—my usual confidants—are as pressured as I am.

Jude continues to listen to these lamentations and offers her own evidence in our discussions. It is in these varying moods of mine that I grasp thankfully at the stability of our love.

November 6

Had lunch this noon with John Stimmel, a young lawyer in town who seems genuinely devoted to his vocation. I have been toying with the idea of going to law school next year, and I wanted to hear the inside story from someone who appears to be enveloped with that life. John was quite honest about the various aspects of his practice, and I left the meal feeling more confused about my own motivation than before. The trouble is, I want to remain in my present situation—or at least what it has been in the past—even as I watch the church finances wither around me.

An angel of mercy visited my office this afternoon. Without warning, Earl, the university psychiatrist, arrived at my door to say that he wanted to talk with me. He had been to the "Associates" meeting last night, and he said that he was extremely concerned about me.

Earl said that I appeared to be totally depressed—that I was obviously anxious during the meeting—that all of this was really none of his business, but he is worried about me.

For no rational reason, I cried. The anxiety of the past two months seemed to gush out without control—and Earl sat quietly as I let it flow. Toward the end of my catharsis, he began to speak very quietly:

"Tom, you are in the process of screwing up your life. You are basically a creative person who works best 'on the street' rather than in an upholstered chair. Whatever artistry you have to offer people is being subdued and destroyed by the administrative busywork of finances and shuffling papers. You are stuck in this building as never before, and this isn't where you belong.

"I realized again last night, Tom, that you and Fred are very opposite type people, with different gifts to offer in different ways. Everyone there last night must have seen the tension in your face, and anyone with any sensitivity at all would know why. You and Fred should not address the same meetings—perhaps you should not even *go* to the same meetings. You two do not complement each other, you detract from each other. That doesn't mean you can't work together in this place and achieve your goals—but don't try to make your relationship with him what it was with Tom Niccolls— that is not fair to him or to you.

"It is my own hang-up that prevented me from talking with you before about this, but after last night I couldn't evade it any longer. I get tied up in my own work, just as you do. But you've got to make a change. Fred or someone else can take over the financial matters—that's not your thing and you know it! You've got to free yourself up. Your worst enemies couldn't have planned a better way to defuse your ministry than you have done yourself. You have taken yourself off the streets where you minister best, and now you are locked in this handsome office, exactly where the reactionary crowd wants you!"

There was little that I could say in response, for I could not comprehend the fact that another person—someone outside of my immediate family and friends—could understand my thoughts and my gut that completely. But perhaps Earl has the same thoughts and the same gut on many occasions. Anyway, I was embarrassed and joyfully thankful for his presence, his concern, his understanding.

As he left my office, we embraced for a moment, and I felt the relief of pressure and the surge of warmth which enters my life when another human being bothers to express the affection of commitment.

The rubber monkey appears now and then.

November 10

I had a long discussion with the staff regarding Earl's visit the other day, and I learned that Fred, too, had a talk with Earl.

We tried to work out a few changes in work responsibility, and Fred agreed to take over many of the financial aspects. I felt rather guilty about that, for no one on the staff should have to do that stuff—it's a matter for the Board to handle. But Fred will end up doing it, I know.

The communication wasn't terribly good today, although Don worked hard at trying to interpret what Fred and I were saying to each other. It's a crazy way to try to communicate, but it was the only thing available to us, I guess. If I were in Fred's place, I would certainly resent the sudden change, and I think he does, but we aren't talking about it very well.

Maybe that's the problem: Fred and I both seem so confused about the present and the future that we are afraid to open up to each other—afraid that our anger will consume us.

November 11

There is an uneasy quietness on this campus, and in this town, but it is a quietness which unfortunately belies what is happening in the lives of the people in this place.

In a sense, the quietness is welcome to the battered minds and hearts of our community, both academic and civic. The new rhetoric has grown old, and the old rhetoric has decayed beyond recognition or interest. Indeed, we must look else-where for those elusive feelings called "community" and "brotherhood" and "hope." We must admit that change involves hard work, footwork, research, commitment, variety in our efforts, and not just slogans.

The quietness which we are in, though, is a lie. Our ministry has become almost totally crisis-oriented this year, and the situation is deteriorating with every day. Our contacts with people who live in the dorms and who live around town only confirm what we suspect, and it suggests that we are seeing only the tip of the iceberg.

People are falling apart, in every way imaginable.

A visitor from out of town recently suggested to me that my view is prejudiced because U.C.M. tends to see only the people who are in "critical" situations. That may be very true. And yet, what we see and what we experience is *real,* for people's lives are increasingly encountering dead ends, and there is nothing "quiet" about that.

Perhaps the greatest difficulty about all of this is that we *are* being so very "quiet" about it. So today I sent out a newsletter, just to break the silence, at least a little bit.

November 15

Just returned from the four-day trip to my prep school, Culver, and I have a strong hint that I will never be asked to "appear" there again. Don and Carolyn Bubenzer and Mike Kulczycki went with Judy and me to help with the "religious conference," and I think that they were rather spooked by the general atmosphere.

The conference itself went pretty well—we used the same multimedia presentation that we have used in the dorms this year, and I think that some messages got through to the cadets and students from other prep schools. Who knows?

We carried along a box full of the "Celebrate Life" buttons that I've had printed for U.C.M., and the cadets seemed most interested in those—although they were told that they couldn't wear them on their uniforms! I guess that the exclamation of life would clash too much with the military insignia . . .

I had been invited to preach in the Sunday chapel service, and I decided to lay it on the cadets about their view of life—about not getting too brainwashed by the militaristic side of things. I mentioned that I had been considered as a real "success" at Culver because I was a true believer, a cadet captain, an asset to the cause. I didn't deride that in my sermon, but suggested that there were other cadets during my era who were certainly as "successful" as I as human beings (some more so), although they didn't have as many stripes or honors as I.

Toward the end of the sermon, I emphasized that we are *all* the children of God, and that we must be aware of our acts of killing in the world. I suggested that perhaps the Christ child would be born on the twenty-fifth of next month in Vietnam rather than in Bethlehem—and perhaps our bombs would destroy the manger . . .

Most of the cadets were most affectionate to all of us, but it was apparent after the chapel service that the administration was extremely upset with my works. The new superintendent, a general, told me that I was simply a bitter young man. I thanked him for his hospitality.

The chaplain—a nice guy who is caught between the gospel and the screaming eagles—told me later that I would not be invited to speak in the chapel again, without doubt.

There are so many good things about the school—it's sad that the chiefs get so uptight when a different point of view is presented, especially in a building which is ostensibly dedicated to the Prince of Peace.

I received an envelope from Chet Marshall, a gentle man who manages to bridge two worlds by being an athletic coach and a sensitive teacher. He spends many hours writing verse, and he and his beautiful wife, Glenda, offered a lengthy poem to us, a poem which celebrated our visit to their lives.

To know that Chet and Glenda are there offering themselves to young minds and hearts made me realize that my trip to Culver and the message which I so vainly wanted to carry concerning love was really not needed, for it exists in the flesh and blood of at least two mortals.

But I would have driven twice that far anyway, just to receive that unexpected envelope.

November 20

Amid the constant demands of problem-pregnancy counseling, and with the approval of Dr. Mattmiller, I met this noon with the Health Center staff, so that I might explain our counseling objectives and listen to any complaints which they might have. I knew ahead of time that there were at least two doctors who were extremely antiabortion and less than thrilled with me and the U.C.M. philosophy.

After my presentation of the alternatives which we suggest to each of our clients, I decided to let the antagonistic doctors yell at me, to vent their feelings, to get it all out now. I made very little response to them as they carried on for several minutes, for I felt that their charges were not connected with our format but with a few of the commercially oriented agencies in New York. I assured the staff that our agency in Manhattan was a nonprofit clinic, and that we were only asking the staff to give young women an official report slip on the results of the pregnancy tests. I also emphasized that some women, after our counseling, decide *not* to have an abortion.

Earl called me later to say that the meeting had been very positive, and he expected increased cooperation.

November 21

A letter from Tom Niccolls, regarding my newsletter of last week:

Dear Tom,

We were really sorry to miss you when we got to Athens. It was good to see Don & Jerry & Judy, tho, & get caught up on UCM involvements, pains & pleasures. There are many things I'd like to see & hear, but pen & paper aren't good means, so I'll forfeit the attempt.

I do know the problem is much more acute than we thought possible and can imagine that it gives you, particularly, a headache. I'm not much of one to counsel equanimity under such circumstances, since I'm a notorious worrier, but I do hope your sense of Yes will bear you up in the midst of the chorus of No's you often hear. Read some Calvinism—if only to make your pulse beat stronger.

I guess the other thing that I got from your newsletter is the feeling of being overwhelmed by the multitudes—something that I felt more than once during our years in Athens. I read the letter in almost apocalyptic categories—and of course there are many others who see our world & our portion of it in those quite biblical terms. But I want to have it be a full-orbed apocalyptic—with as strong a sense of the Throne as well as the Four Horsemen. That's why William Stringfellow's recent article in *Christian Century* meant so much to me—the reality of death-idolatory & the possibility of resurrection.

Does the God talk only bruise you more? You know I don't want it to, but you know that's what I'm ultimately driven to when all the rest of the easy intellectualisms drop away—so translate it into your own style—but know above all, I'm trying to say I love your willingness to be real and faithful & may all the hippie Confessors & Saints and the Root of our dignity stand beside you! Oh damn, I miss you.

love,
Tom

P.S. Buy a rubber monkey.

I have a very strong feeling that rubber monkeys aren't bought. They simply fall out of pockets at the most unexpected times, bringing relief and hope. I hope one falls again soon.

November 23

This afternoon I was visited by a woman from the Lutheran church, who wanted to check into our counseling practices. She wanted to know if we are "presenting Jesus" to the young people as we counsel them. I told her that I didn't know what she was talking about, but I assumed that Jesus was present whenever people try to be loving and accepting and concerned about each other. But she wanted to know if we "direct the young people to the Bible." I told her that I rarely mention the Bible in *any* counseling, for it is rarely mentioned by my clients. I added the opinion that most of these young people have been thumped on the head with the Bible all of their lives, and then generally ignored by the Church.

"Then do you mention the need for forgiveness for the young women who become pregnant out of wedlock?"

I mentioned that we often talk about guilt feelings, but that I do not insist that the individual ask Jesus for absolution. I am usually more concerned about the existential guilt which is heaped on the young woman whose parents call her a two-bit whore.

"What then makes this place different than any other agency—what makes it uniquely *Christian?*"

Only that we are supported financially and morally by a group of Christian churches. We on the staff happen to call ourselves Christians and try to live out that life-style as we understand it. Therefore, we are not any more unique than the Christian who is working at any other job.

She was generally rather nice, but I think that she left with great disappointment over our approach—and a bit scandalized by our actions.

November 24

A young woman—who worked so hard in the Draft Office last year, who could be so gently loving and so fearfully distant, who can stroke the world or strike it with equal abandon, who seems to be constantly searching while damning the search, who is now trying to find some hope and accomplishment in a community-service program in another state—sent a letter today which included the seemingly ubiquitous emotions of despair and frustration which I see around me constantly these days.

What in the hell are you telling or asking, my dear friend?

Is it simply what we are all feeling in this winter of hesitation and confusion: that hope is a premium item, not easily found in the quiet chaos? I must keep believing that we don't *have* to be destroyed—by others or by ourselves. And yet, I don't know how to tell her that, via air mail, so I won't bother. But I would like to *embrace* her, for even a moment, to tell her *that* way.

November 25

In a meeting with the university vice-president, concerning my crisis newsletter, I was told that things really aren't that bad—I am simply seeing the "most upset" of the students, and, consequently, there is no need for unusual concern. Everything will be all right . . .

I think that the meeting was intended to accomplish two things: first, to inform me that I really don't know what the hell I'm talking about and, secondly, to quietly suggest that the "emergency center" idea is going to go nowhere at this time.

Okay.

Happy Thanksgiving . . .

November 27

Such a beautiful thing happened.

I have been doing some premarital counseling with a couple, and it has gotten rather complicated because of hostility in the bride's family—anger and guilt over things in the past which are carried on rather than forgotten. It has been an emotional ordeal for all involved, and the girl's father decided not to come to the wedding at all.

In the midst of the wedding at U.C.M. this afternoon, as I was preparing to introduce the vows, the bride's mother arose from her chair, walked over to the couple, and quietly embraced each of them.

It was so unexpected and so gentle.

I tried to ignore that demanding lump that arises in my throat at such moments, but I was rather overwhelmed.

Perhaps only the daughter knew what it *really* means.

November 30

A little reverse spin on the normal pitch.

A local citizen came to see me today because his son is becoming a problem—it seems that the kid is hanging around with the "Jesus people" on campus. The man felt that the kid is being brainwashed (probably true) with some strange beliefs (the Gospel?), and he wants me to check into the group to see if dope is being used.

Although I often get uptight with the narcissistic approach of the "Young Life" advocates, I hardly believe that they are using "dope" to convince anyone to join.

I'm not so sure that I would want my own teen-ager in the "Jesus" movement either, but it seems to me that it beats hell out of some of the other things going on nowadays. I wonder what a kid can do around here that won't catch hell from mom and dad?

"Repent!" the kids say—and that scares the hell out of us —almost as much as "Give peace a chance . . ."

"I want you to be a good Christian, Johnny, but don't get too serious about it."

December 1

I met briefly with the representative of the "Young Life" group this afternoon, and told him that some parents were pretty uptight about the activities of the group. I don't think he was too surprised, for he said that he would try to talk to them as he had with others.

The occasion gave me an opportunity to express my own biases against the group, mainly in terms of some guys who had come in for counseling last year. It seems that these fellows had been "led on" by a couple of the girls in the "Jesus group," and then hit with the line, "Well, Charlie, if you really want to keep going with me, you'll have to accept Jesus into your life." I thought that it was a pretty cheap way of trying to get "converts," and this fellow agreed with me—he said he didn't know anything about the incident, which is probably true. But *someone* gave those girls the idea that they had to gain converts one way or another.

At the conclusion of the meeting, we decided to let each other do his own thing. And I asked him to tell the group to quit praying for the salvation of *my* soul at their public pray-ins, for I believed that Christ had taken care of that several hundred years ago.

He departed with a smile on his face, suggesting that he was silently praying for the salvation of my soul . . .

December 4

One of the limitations in stereotyping people is that we sometimes miss the exciting events in their lives.

I had lunch with a faculty member who wanted to talk with me about the activities of U.C.M., and I knew that he was not in sympathy with much that we do. I guess that I had him pretty well categorized in my mind.

As he was giving me a lengthy description of his back-ground over a tuna salad, I discovered to my amazement that he had been a fellow prisoner of war in Germany with my literary hero, Kurt Vonnegut, Jr. He gave me a precise ac-count of their adventures there, of the tremendous pressures which were exerted on Vonnegut, of the factors which surely affected Vonnegut's later writings. I was mesmerized by the poignant narrative, hungrier for the episodes in Vonnegut's past than for the Reuben sandwich on my plate. This pro-fessor was telling me all of this so that I would understand that he had come out of the experiences in Germany with a different point of view from Vonnegut—and he felt that U.C.M. was going a bit overboard in its opposition to Vietnam and other issues.

The man was tremendously honest with me, and I ap-preciated his willingness to talk—and so I tried to treat him with respect. But, as respectfully as I could, I told him that I thought the Vietnam situation was and is an incredible ob-scenity to our national life, that we will be hated throughout Asia for decades because of napalm-and-bombs diplomacy, that we cannot justify the megadeaths by the specious argument that the "other side" is doing the same thing.

I concluded my observations with the suggestion that the Church is called to judgment for its silence in this matter—and that he might not have experienced that prison camp if the German ministers had spoken out more forcefully in the thirties, rather than blessing the bombs and ovens of Adolf Hitler.

He tacitly agreed, but I do not think he was convinced.

December 7

A weeping coed came to see me late this afternoon, and I shuddered at her story.

She has been going with a guy rather steadily, and she liked him a great deal, although he is heavily into the drug culture, something she has not joined.

A week ago, he gave her a drink at his apartment, and she soon discovered that the drink had been laced with LSD. She learned an hour ago that he had stripped her and taken pictures of various parts of her body while she was tripping—he now plans to sell the pictures to someone in another state, and some of the pictures have her face in them.

I worked for awhile to quiet her down, and then made the following suggestion: that she tell him of my knowledge of the situation, adding that I am ready to notify the state and federal authorities if he does not give her the negatives and/or if he should threaten or hurt her in any way.

From the experiences in Detroit, Jersey, and Athens, I should have learned by now about the savagery of human beings, but I still find myself horrified by the things that one person is willing to do to another.

December 9

Two years ago today, the surprise and quickness of death was visited upon Thomas Merton, the searching Trappist monk, known to his silent brothers as M. Louis. I have felt an affinity with Merton for a long time, not only because of his attempt to see beyond the narrowness of Western theology, but also because of a personal matter: his friends were as puzzled by his entry into the religious as mine were by my ordination.

Since the time of Merton's death, I have attempted to go back to his writings and his life, to embrace him when I can, to argue against his early narrow orthodoxy when I must, to remind myself again that he is gone.

Perhaps more than anything else, I carry with me the beginning statement of his "A Devout Meditation in Memory of Adolph Eichmann":

> One of the most disturbing acts that came out in the Eichmann trial was that a psychiatrist examined him and pronounced him *perfectly sane.* I do not doubt it at all, and that is why I find it disturbing. The sanity of Eichmann is disturbing. We equate sanity with a sense of justice, with humaneness, with prudence, with the capacity to love and understand other people. We rely on the sane people of the world to preserve it from barbarism, madness, destruction. And it now begins to dawn on us that it is precisely the *sane* ones who are the most dangerous.
>
> It is the sane ones, the well-adapted ones, who can without qualms and without nausea aim the missiles and press the buttons that will initiate the great festival of destruction that they, *the sane ones,* have prepared. . . . No one suspects the sane, and the sane ones will have *perfectly good reasons,* logical well-adjusted reasons, for firing the (atomic) shot. They will be obeying sane orders that have come sanely down the chain of command. And because of their sanity they will have no qualms at all. When the missiles take off, then, *it will be no mistake. . . .* Eichmann was

sane. The generals and fighters on both sides, in World War II, the ones who carried out the total destruction of entire cities, these were the sane ones. Those who have invented and developed atomic bombs, thermonuclear bombs, missiles; who have planned the strategy of the next war; who have evaluated the various possibilities of using bacterial and chemical agents: these are not the crazy people, they are the sane people. The ones who cooly estimate how many millions of victims can be considered expendable in a nuclear war, I presume they do all right with the Rorschach ink blots too. On the other hand, you will probably find that the pacifists and the ban-the-bomb people are, quite seriously just as we read in *Time,* a little crazy. (*Ramparts,* October, 1966, vol. 5, no. 4.)

"Crazy" Thomas Merton died in an absurd manner: he was in Thailand, continuing his studies of Eastern religions; he took a bath one hot afternoon, and he touched a short-circuited electric fan. He was instantly electrocuted.

The saints die in odd ways.

Celebrate the craziness.

I miss you, Brother M. Louis.

December 11

More thoughts tonight about vocation. What can I become an expert at? But what the hell is an expert?

When we entered Vietnam, we decided to leave it to the *experts,* both diplomatic and military: now, we are experts at death.

We dramatically entered the ghettos in the early sixties, asking the *experts* to unravel the despair and poverty, and the "Great Society" became a hollow shibboleth.

The Church always sought the *experts* who could mumble the magic words, until someone discovered that the magic was not in the expert but in the celebrant; and now we try to make "expert celebrants" out of the laity.

Once overrun by the *experts* of analytic interpretation, the field of psychology began to breathe some fresh air in the form of commonsense approaches to everyday problems; now we are fervently searching for experts in common sense, lest we look too unscientific.

Our *experts* in prison design speak to us from hallways strewn with burning debris and inmate corpses.

Our *experts* in human relations look out at us from the crowds of an alienated society.

Our media *experts* sell us the all-meat dogfood during commercials on the six o'clock news, while that same news film expertly shows us the starvation of ten thousand people on a given day.

Why do *I* want to be an expert *too?*

So I'll be accepted.

So I'll be judged "sane."

December 12

This is Jude's birthday, and that birth did much to make my life as complete as it is. Are there any new ways to tell her how totally I love her?

She listens for hours to my rantings and questions, knowing that eventually I will be back to where I started, ranting even more. Sometimes she listens by knitting or staring through a fantasy or looking in my eyes or peering through the Marlboro smoke or cleaning off the kitchen table or fixing some instant coffee. But she is listening.

Her responses come softly and only occasionally, for she is usually thinking what I am saying, and the communion lies in the same questions, however imperfectly answered by both of us.

She has listened and spoken and comforted and challenged me for ten years now, and when the conversations reach their final uncertainties, I usually ask her our private joke: "Well, Jude, what does it all mean?"

She then puts her arm around my neck, brings her smile close to my cheek, and says ritually, "Like I told ya before, fella, I just don't know . . ."

What sort of birthday gift is there for the deepest love I have ever known?

December 18

I continue to have seemingly incessant thoughts about further training for some other vocation. The messages we continue to get concerning future funding here are bleak, and I do not imagine that there will be more than a one-man staff in two years. I do not want to be the last guy here—I don't think I could go it alone.

Doctor, lawyer, Indian chief? I sound like an adolescent, trying to figure out my life's work. But we are in a new age, and there are going to be constant vocational decisions for millions.

I have considered medicine on and off for the past ten years, but friends keep telling me that I don't have the scientific background to try it at this point in life. They're probably right, but it still nags at me. The law seems to be the main option now, even though my enthusiasm for it wanes considerably, but I have taken the Law School Admission Test, just to be sure.

I wonder if anyone else in the world feels in control of his life?

VII

Rosewater said an interesting thing to Billy one time about a book that wasn't science fiction. He said that everything there was to know about life was in **The Brothers Karamazov,** by Fyodor Dostoevsky. "But that isn't **enough** any more," said Rosewater.

—Kurt Vonnegut, Jr.,
Slaughterhouse-Five

January 5, 1971

Why do I—and obviously so *many* of my acquaintances— appear to be so uncertain, searching, discredited, unqualified, and desperate in our goals these days?

How can we demand reformation of institutions, and then —being ignored—expect to find meaningful lives in institutions?

How can we vehemently protest the power of certification in the hands of small groups of men—and then ask for certification from them?

Am I so weak as to be unable to find an acceptable place in my world without a new title, another degree, a sign on the door, or an *official* pat on the back?

How did Thoreau or any of the other giants manage to do it?

Why do I think of the *giants?* Have my perceptions of reality been denied so many times by my government, by my

Church, by my community that I envision myself as a pygmy of worth?

Why do I deny the poet's advice of living by the side of the road and being a friend to Man?

Ironically, irately, irrationally, I continue to grope for the slightest possibilities, discovering only, it seems, that I grope along with endless others.

For the past two days, I have been meeting with a group of young clergy in Columbus. It was a private affair, and the guys flew into Columbus from their jobs in parishes all over the country. I was one of the oldest of the eleven, and one of the few who didn't have a regular parish position.

The intent of the discussion was to find out where the Church is headed—what each of us sees going on at this point —sharing some perceptions of what might be a viable ministry in the near and distant future. After a great deal of "shop-talk" and general disagreement, we decided to project a fantasy of an organization which would meet the various needs of the members of a certain community—in terms of programs, resources, talents, goals, and all the rest. The idea was to expand our minds and priorities and assumptions to a point where we might be able to see some new trends and possibilities.

As with most human experiences with fantasy, we soon got too tied up in reality, and the last several hours of discussion evolved into an immense theory on how all of us could form an "intentional community" somewhere, with each of us performing a different function for the community. Of course, we decided that it would take a few years of planning and training, for several of us would have to go back to school to get the necessary credentials. In the midst of the "fantasy of reality," I volunteered to be the community lawyer!

Some really effective and bright young men of the Church were in attendance. And we really didn't get anywhere. It wasn't a waste of time, actually, for several of us saw the limited nature of our exercise, and that's an important learning in itself. But we made the mistake of thinking that we could design a community which would be superimposed on a larger community somewhere else—and that simply won't work. If we are going to offer anything in terms of renewal in the church, we will have to do it in our own "place," wherever that may be, using the resources of the people who live there too.

Another fellow and I stated very directly that we felt that there was simply not enough time in the immediate future to plan for some community in three or five years. The pressures and demands of this present world are upon us *now*. There was some underlying hostility toward us for our "pessimism" in the project, and, upon my departure, I realized that I, for one, would not be an integral part of the future planning of the group.

It was enjoyable and exciting to be with some interesting minds for a couple of days—but distressing to see that we could not perceive beyond the renewal possibilities of three years ago.

January 6

The Epiphany is a celebration of the declaration of Christ's existence to the world. It is a minor day in the normal observation of the Church calendar—but it is the anniversary of my ordination to the priesthood. For some reasons which are only dimly apparent to me, this is an important day in my life each year. But I share that fact with no one, until, perhaps, now.

Don has had a difficult situation with a problem-pregnancy case, one which shows the benighted attitudes of some of our medical brothers, as well as our clients.

A woman from the very rural area of this county came to see Don because she is about twenty weeks pregnant, and she does not think she can handle another child, either emotionally or financially. She is in her early twenties and already has had five children! She comes from an extremely poor family, and there has been little effort to get any birth-control education to her tiny community.

The woman did have enough concern about herself and her family to ask the doctor to perform a tubal ligation after the last birth. His response? "Oh, now we don't want to do something like that—you'll probably want to have some more children someday in the future!" What hope is there in trying to change community attitudes when a *doctor*—with at least eight years college education—lays out a rap like that?

After a few days' work, Don has arranged an appointment with a doctor in New York for the woman—but all of us are extremely uptight about the length of the pregnancy.

Fred has been expressing a great deal of anxiety about the problem-pregnancy counseling situation, and he does not want to deal personally with any women who are over twelve weeks pregnant. Intellectually, I don't blame him one bit, for we *all* are anxious about that issue—but his decision seems to add more pressure to my own gut, for I feel that Don and I will have to take all of those cases from now on. It is really not our choice, for the women know that the New York law exists, and we have said that we will be counselors.

Internally, I resent Fred's decision, but he probably resented the fact that I dumped all of the financial worries on him a couple of months ago.

We are not working so much as a staff but as a group of individuals who happen to be in the same building, groping for cooperative efforts, but finding little direction. Communication between Fred and me is superficial. Don and Rosie Wood, our secretary, try to fill in the gaps of understanding, but it isn't working terribly well. Fred and I are not facing each other directly, and I don't understand it myself.

We are afraid of each other—but why?

January 18

At the Board meeting tonight, it was decided to raise the salaries for Fred and me very slightly because the money is so obviously short. The group also decided to hire Don for another year, assuming that some finances are available.

It wasn't a very happy group . . .

January 19

Each year the students are allowed to cast votes for the professors whom they think are the best teachers in the university. A committee then takes these nominations and chooses five "University Professors," each of whom receive an extra thousand dollars in salary and the right to teach any course he or she designs. It has been a positive program in the sense of rewarding good teaching, while simultaneously giving the student population a voice in their own community.

One of the profs so nominated this year, Warner Montgomery in the College of Education, has recently been informed by the Dean of that College that he is being put on a terminal contract, for reasons unknown. There are thousands of rumors passing through the halls of various academic and civic buildings, but the general consensus is that Warner is simply "too advanced" in his ideas on education to suit the rather old-style concepts of the College. His critics suggest sotto voce that Warner is somehow corrupting the morals of young students!

I have been to two of Montgomery's classes, and I found the presentation and discussion to be unusually open and deliberate. The students were allowed to disagree with him and with each other—and that afforded some rather exciting debates. One of the classes discussed "corporal punishment" in schools, and it was beneficial, I think.

I sent out a letter to the Board members today, asking them to sign a petition in support of Montgomery's continued employment at the university. I don't really give his case much chance, but we must respond in some manner to the viewpoint which is so often expressed in the College of Education.

January 20

In the past several weeks, there have been two babies born to coeds in the dorms. The first was born on November 30th, and the child lived through the ordeal. The second, born yesterday, died, for the girl panicked and tried to hide the event from the dorm authorities.

God, it is such a pathetic situation. Earl told me that he talked with the girl last night, and she is terribly naïve about the whole situation—passive and frightened—he thinks that she honestly didn't know how far along she was—she muttered something about five months!

Once more I would plead for sex education, but the high schools and colleges treat it like leprosy.

January 22

By action of an administrative committee, any immediate plans for the crisis center have been canceled and we shall continue to assume that personal needs are being met effectively on campus.

Recently I was called to a dormitory by a distraught resident director who informed me that the girls in the dorm had become overwhelmed by fear of the "supernatural." What started earlier as an innocent interest in a Ouija board had degenerated into a nightly ritual of investigating "the spirits of the dead" and assorted other subjects.

It was all very humorous until one girl began seeing her deceased father sitting on her bed. Another girl was on the point of tears incessantly, and several girls were demanding to have the overhead lights on all night. The dorm seemed to be in a state of shock.

I discovered without too much trouble that the focal point of these events was one girl, and she appeared to me as someone who needed rather extensive counseling. She was in desperate need of attention, I thought, and willing to do about anything to get it. Because of my own personal link with the "supernatural" in the priesthood, I felt that I was not the one to discuss the issue with the dorm residents, so I called Mike Hanek, director of the Center for Psychological Services, who could approach the women as a "scientist."

Unfortunately, this is not an "unusual" event on campus, and I think that it reflects some of the bizarre things going on.

The administration says that everything will be all right.

January 24

I had been invited to speak to the "adults" at Hillel, the Jewish campus center, this morning, and so I told them of some of my personal pressures and concerns for the future. I wasn't too optimistic about many things, but they tried to respond, and it was a good exchange—at least for me.

I told them that I envied their tradition of religious and cultural expression, and that I missed that sort of thing in the Christian Church. Most of them suggested that it was dying within their community, too, and I found that unfortunate.

I would love to have a "tradition" to hold on to in my personal life, something I could believe in as a positive myth. But most of the traditions I see in this nation and in this Church are those which effectively separate people into opposing groups, with little understanding or acceptance of others.

Recently I saw a television show which included some words about an Indian burial ground—about how the Indians revere the soil as holy. I felt a deep sense of envy as I watched the show, for I wanted very much to believe in something like that—to revere an object of community sacredness—but I realized that the "sacred" in my own life is of a more transitory nature—I revere the relationships which I have with certain people—they carry me along in hope and love—but they are too often at a distance from me. The "Jesus freaks" would have me "trust in the Lord," but that is an empty statement unless it is grounded in at least *some* reality.

I heard a television news commentator say once that the media has inadvertently become a myth destroyer. If a person or an event becomes a positive myth in the life of the people, the media will so overreport it and investigate it that sooner or later the myth will be destroyed. He is right.

I think so often of the clown, of the rubber monkey—they

are my myths at the moment, for they give me an absurd hope that there are people who can love and be loved.

January 26

The apparent split in viewpoint on the Warner Montgomery case is evident in our letter to the *Post* today—less than half of the Board and staff signed it. A lot of people don't know enough of the "facts," others obviously agree with the action against Montgomery, and still others are very reticent to express their opinion, one way or another. It is important to me, though, to get this thing discussed, and our printed comments were meant to support Montgomery's concern with the *whole* person . . . but is anyone listening?

January 27

"Jude, we've got to do something," the familiar discussion began.

"I know," she said, lighting a cigarette and reaching for an ashtray to put between us on the bed. "You've looked and sounded tired and confused for weeks now. You need a change —something you can be excited about and involved in."

"Maybe the law thing . . . maybe just go ahead and do the lawyer trip."

She smiled at me gently before the self-evident reply: "You don't sound too enthused with that one." There was a cigarette-long silence.

My recurring fantasy found words: "You know what would really be neat? To be a doctor in a semirural area—you know, with a city not too far away—but sort of a country area— maybe in Appalachia somewhere, and have a clinic, work with a couple of other crazy doctors. That sounds so nice . . ."

I stared at the ceiling, and I knew that Jude was looking at me. I feel good when she is looking at me.

"But I probably couldn't even get *into* med school, much less become the Appalachian Albert Schweitzer," I said smiling. "Hey, how about a newspaper? We could borrow some money from the family, buy some small weekly, hire a few staffers from the *Post,* raise hell over some local issues . . . and go broke in a matter of weeks!"

"Okay . . . sounds good," she answered. I knew that she was ready to agree to almost anything.

"Or we could go into film work . . . or buy a small radio station . . . or I could try to write the Mediocre American Novel . . . or . . ." Some silence followed.

"Tom?"

"Yeah?"

"What do you *want* to do?"

"Everything. Nothing. I don't know."

"I thought so," she said forgivingly.

"But I do know one thing: we ought to announce to the community that we're leaving U.C.M., that I'm going to get some further training in something . . . I'll ask the *Post* to print something . . . I'll think of something to say . . . and then, with the story out, I'll *have* to get my act together . . . then I'll *have* to find something else to do."

"Okay," she said, and she meant it.

"You know, it's really been a good place to live . . . the area . . . all the people at the house all the time . . . the Friday nights of group pizza and watching 'Chiller' on the tube . . . and all the other stuff."

She smiled and nodded.

"And I love the hell out of you, woman."

The lights went out.

January 29

The *Post* printed a large article about our decision today, and I am glad that it is out in the open. The article was complimentary, but I think that our personal comments evidenced our own indecision as to where we are going and what we plan to do. I suggested that our plans would deal "primarily with the possibility of law school or multimedia journalism" —but those were offered only to fill in the embarrassing gaps of uncertainty.

February 3

A deeply personal, loving letter today from Tom Niccolls, regarding the article in the *Post* last Friday about the future departure of the Jacksons, ended with this quote:

> "Somebody placed the shuttle in your hand:
> somebody who had already arranged the threads."
>
> Hammarskjöld

Weave well.

peace,
Tom

I wonder, Tom Niccolls, if I would be planning to leave Athens if you were still here. I wonder if I will ever again work with someone who understands my thoughts almost before I think them, or with whom my personality and hopes and quirks mesh so well. You and your crazy Calvinism!

If this is truly the Age of Anxiety as Auden describes it, then I begin to think that the anxiety comes from our constant departures one from another. We occasionally find that human being with whom we can share so much of life, and before the celebration of it can get very far, we move on to another place, and our relationships are then carried by postage stamps and weary mailmen.

Why in hell do we leave? Are we driven by some sort of "success" motive which demands that we scamper up the ladder of fame and profit, regardless of what and whom we leave behind? Do we move on simply because we are out of control, pushed on by the very mobility of our society, moving because everyone else is moving? Or is this one of those Big Lessons in Life that I am supposed to learn: to grow is to move, to move is to grow.

I wonder if the article in the paper last week was really, finally a fraud. I don't know why I want to move. I simply know that I don't want to be left *alone* in this job, facing all of these people without support and hope and rest. That is cowardice, I suppose.

Maybe I'm leaving, or at least trying to leave, only because of cowardice.

February 7

One of the more consistent aspects of my life is being told that I won't be invited back to preach somewhere. So it happened at the Presbyterian church this morning—and I think that I was lucky to get out with my scalp!

I reflected on a few of my experiences in the church—some of them being the clichés which so many ministers experience, but as Edgar Whan says, "You know you're getting old when you realize that most of the clichés are true."

I said that we would probably get more upset over a brick through one of the stained-glass windows than we would with the continuing *deaths* of adults and children throughout the world.

I said that God was probably very bored with our Sunday-morning pieties, and that we should allow the little children to lead us in worship with their balloons and gaiety, for we have been told that theirs is the understanding of the Kingdom of God.

I said—when a woman stood up and walked out in the middle of my sermon—that we should be happy with such honest expression of feeling in our liturgy.

I said that the Gospel—when truly believed and acted upon —would divide families and universities and towns into opposing views of priorities—just as it is happening in these present days.

I said—probably—too much.

The sermon itself divided the congregation into two major views: those who liked the ideas, and those who thought I spoke sacrilege.

The choir—which usually sings a series of angelic "amens" at the end of the weekly sermon—sang nothing at the conclusion of mine.

One big wheel from the university told me that I was "bitter" in my viewpoint—his wife said that she really enjoyed the sermon. I bet they had a wonderful afternoon together!

The woman who had invited me to speak was surrounded by irate critics throughout the "social hour" after the service, and I knew that they were forcing some sort of blood vow on her never to invite me back.

The parish is getting ready to put in new carpeting and to sandblast the outside of the building—all of it for about six thousand dollars—so they will soon forget what I had to say.

Tom Niccolls, as usual, was right in something he said last year. He said that the basic "strength" of any institution— and especially the Church—is that it can *absorb* and finally ignore any real criticism. After all of the upsetness of any event, it will finally go back to the trivialties.

Maybe that's a pretty good description of all of us.

February 10

There was a small gathering on the College Green to protest the continuing obscenity of the war—including a couple of short speeches and some "street theater" about the atrocities in Nam—but few people watched or cared. Business went on as usual—as usual.

Any institution can finally absorb and ignore.

February 15

The annual "inspection team" checked out the U.C.M. operation and presented its findings to the Board at a meeting at our house tonight.

Everything was very polite and cordial, and the only obvious criticism suggested that we need a "more rigorous process of setting priorities."

That's probably very accurate—but I don't know the answer to it. Like ministries everywhere, if we say and do the things that need to be said and done, we're just going to be called "commies" and get a taste of that rail out of town—and then we'll spend all of our time *explaining* why we did something or other! Or we can spend all of our time trying to meet the counseling needs of this population—eventually burning ourselves out mentally, and living with the guilt of ignoring the social needs.

Oh, there's no damned reason for us to feel sorry for ourselves, but we do! If this era is going to continue to be as hec-

tic and demoralizing and confusing as it has been for the past
few years, then we had better just get used to it and live
through it, celebrating each day at a time.

But it's hard to set priorities. And as Harvey Cox says,
"Not to decide is to decide."

February 23

A young woman stopped in to talk about an abortion—
she didn't want to discuss any other possibilities. I found out
that this will be her *third*—she didn't seem to care, and she
won't take the pill.

Maybe she can't face the guilt of really caring, but I was
angry as hell!

March 6

Would you believe that a girl would get pregnant with her
best friend's *father?*

And would you believe that the best friend originally set
up several of the dates for her father?

And would you believe that the father is not divorced yet
from the mother?

And that none of the parties involved seem to think that
this is a rather "unusual" situation?

Would you believe that the girl has no money—and the
father is not too wild about sending her to New York because
it costs too much?

It's all true.

I was so damned depressed after talking with the girl—
who is pretty and gentle and confused and seemingly more

interested in astrology than in her situation—that I came home early and just stared at a wall for a couple of hours.

I sometimes totally lack comprehension of this world I live in—and then I think that *I'm* the crazy one, and I get concerned about my mental health.

What *is* reality anymore?

March 11

Reality diminishes even more . . .

Bill Black, the Episcopal rector in town, called this afternoon to tell me that he had a counseling case he wanted to bring over to my office. Okay.

The guy with Bill was about twenty-eight, I'd say, and he began talking as soon as the two of them sat down.

He said that he had been traveling through the *fourth dimension,* where he had been taken as a prisoner by another civilization from outer space.

I began to wonder if this was a sick joke, but I soon realized that no one was laughing—and that this guy had a brilliant mind; he had graduated from O.U. several years ago.

He informed me that he was a representative of "Teh Industries," which was the name used on earth by this extraterrestrial group. The guy even had a *brochure* with his name on it, a brochure which offered various "services" to the prospective client . . .

Where the hell am I? I looked at my desk for several seconds, just to make sure in my own skull that I was awake and actually sitting in my office on earth!

The guy laid out a grid of objects on the floor—sixteen items in all, ranging from books to pencils to unknown personal objects—and I asked him what that meant.

"Nothing—and everything. It is what it is, as a sign of what we are and will become." He then described his present life: controlled by the outer power, unable to make geographic moves without permission, liable to be called at any time for future work. A slave to the fourth dimension.

I kept looking at objects around the room, hoping for a feeling of reality, noticing that Bill was saying absolutely nothing. I wanted to grab his hand for security!

The guy continued with his description of "reality," and I began to understand the meaning of schizophrenia. He seemed to lunge back and forth between the present situation and the fantasy world. I was getting more unsure of my own stability, and I decided to take a chance on a sudden move.

I practically *screamed* out, "My God, you must be terribly, terribly lonely in your life!"

With that, the fellow covered his face with his hands, leaned back on the sofa, and sobbed for several minutes. I knew that I had made some sort of connection in reality, but I still didn't know what I was doing.

He said that his "new life" had brought a separation from his wife and family—that no one understood—that he had been staying in a room at the Ohio University Inn for ten days, with no money to pay for it. The manager had asked him for the money, but he can't pay, and—then he seemed to suddenly change his expression—he can't leave until he has permission from the fourth dimension. And the FBI is watching him . . . and he doesn't know where to go . . . and . . .

After ninety minutes of this, Bill said that he would try to help the fellow with the money problem, and I gave Bill a look which said silently, "It will take more than money, brother!" Bill understood.

Back and forth the guy went from one aspect of his personality to another, and I was never absolutely sure where he was—with us or back in a time warp.

As he left my office with Bill—having collected his grid of

reality back into his briefcase—he said that he better go see his shrink. Amen, brother.

I came home, again, and sat alone for awhile. The experience shattered me. I wonder how an attractive, bright human being goes off the deep end like that. I wonder if it could happen to me. I wonder what happens inside when you can no longer look at familiar objects and know that they are "reality."

I wonder why Bill brought the guy to *my* office . . .

March 12

My fantasies about the possibility of medical school have increased lately, and I've sought advice from several people. Jude seems certainly willing to give it a try with me.

Earl, who recounted his own med school and internship memories, says that I'm insane.

Today I had lunch with Harry Chovnick out at the mental hospital, for I knew that he had entered med school in his early thirties—and I guess I needed some morale boosting.

Harry—in his animated, deliriously real conversation—finally said simply that a person does "what he has to do, what he *can* do."

"You've got to *touch* life," he said, grabbing my arm. "You've got to *smell* reality," he exclaimed with a forcible inhalation through his nose. "You've got to keep all of those beautiful senses alive and moving and sensitive. You've got to do any damned old thing you can think of that will keep you *aware* of what's going on *around* you and *in* you and *through* you. goddamnit, Tom, do what you want and stay alive . . . and I'll write you a hell of a good reference for anything!"

I love Harry's passion—and his belief in me.

March 19

An interview at the Ohio State Medical School confirmed my suspicions about a long road ahead! The dean said that I have about eighteen month's worth of premedical study to do before I can even think of applying for the fall of '73. Then three or four years of medical training; then an internship; then a residency; then . . .

I wonder if I can hack all of that!

March 28

Sent out the following letter to the Board:

> As some of you know, I have this insane, irrational, unrealistic desire to go to medical school—a desire that I have disregarded for a long time, mainly because of my age, non-scientific background, and so forth. So, I've started with ten hours of zoology and math this quarter, and plan full time chemistry and physics starting in the summer. Strange.
>
> Naturally, I had hoped to continue full time at UCM while doing all of this during the next year, but that is simply impossible.
>
> Therefore, I am asking the Board to allow me to go on "academic leave" this quarter, to terminate my financial contract as it has been, and to decide what I might be paid for the work I have remaining at UCM.
>
> Thanks for your consideration . . . and for accepting the confusion of the past six months. If I work for 18 months and don't get in to med school—well, back to the drawing board.

VIII

It's really a wonder that I haven't dropped all my ideals, because they seem so absurd and impossible to carry out. Yet I keep them because in spite of everything I still believe that people are really good at heart.

—Anne Frank

April 3, 1971

I'm back tonight from a Board conference at Lake Hope.

Back from rented cabins, from twenty-four hour dialogues, from scurrying people attempting to rationally debate elusive issues.

I barter on issues important and mundane. The war. The university. The Church. Salary. Vacation.

Fred makes subtle and/or bold suggestions about studying in graduate history or—on a long shot—law school.

Don wants another year at U.C.M., but has his eye on graduate work in the Guidance and Counseling Department.

Mike, ditto.

It appears to be a three-ring, mediocre clown act: the Board watching the manic staff discussing future departures; Geoff Wood valiantly trying to make sense out of it all; side discussions on Nixon and Agnew to relieve the immediate tension; group fantasies of LBJ sitting on his Texas porch drawling, "Screw all of you—I got out of the chaos!"; walks in the woods; lengthy laughter of sudden indifference to the entire enterprise; new plans for campus programs; and veiled animosity between many of us, the result of good ol' ubiquitous frustration.

Fred constantly asks me if his presence and actions this year have somehow forced me out of U.C.M. I try to convince him that that is not the case—I knew that I had to make a decision about further training at some point, and I might as well do it now. He certainly isn't convinced by my repetitious response—and maybe I'm not too convincing when I say it. Although our relationship is somewhat brittle, he is not "at fault" or the "cause" of what is happening now. There are simply too many financial and social pressures working on all of us—things which are indescribable for us at least.

My brain is in total chaos about the financial issue in my case. Sometimes the staff members say that I shouldn't go on half-salary this quarter, for that will set a precedent for anyone else who wants to take part-time courses in the future. Yet, the vestiges of my Protestant-ethic conscience speak to me loudly and clearly about getting paid for only practical results. Then again, I think that I have been getting paid for a forty-hour week during the past four years in the ministry when, in reality, I have worked eighty-hour weeks consistently. I also know that I can't suddenly cut off my "ministry" even if I want to—my compulsion will certainly force me to take on counseling and related work just because I have trouble saying no.

These thoughts constantly lead to greater confusion—and the increasing confusion leads to further anger or resentment or something negative because there is no resolution to the inner gnawings. So I seek the convenient scapegoat—be it Fred or the Board or myself. I pound away at it internally, satisfying no one, accomplishing nothing.

When my counseling clients mention that sort of thing in their own lives, I tell them that it's sort of dumb, and that they should stop it.

I never have been very good at healing myself.

April 4

On this Palm Sunday, I spoke to the Unitarian Fellowship, and much of the emotion of the past few years seemed to get hold of me and carry me to a public catharsis.

Five years ago on Palm Sunday, I took a flight from seminary to Detroit to be with my father during the last minutes of his life. After a two-year struggle against an insidious blood condition which finally became leukemia, he was unable to fight any longer—there were no more tubes or needles or potions which could induce a miraculous cure.

Two weeks before, when we had our last talk together—when he admitted to me for the first time that he was aware of his terminal condition—he told me of hundreds of the minor/ major, important/trivial, idealistic/pragmatic things which a man—a father—wants to leave behind with his son.

He told me about riding a horse bareback through a rural meadow when he was eleven.

He said that the clerical collar—which I was soon to wear —carried with it a great deal of respect—respect which is often given when it has not been earned by the individual—but given because of historical factors. I must not always assume that I had earned that public respect. "Wear the collar carefully," he said.

He said that he had loved his work and the people in it. No doubts about that. He said that he had met a few buffoons in the steel business, but, on the whole, people were trying to be loving to each other.

He told me that he loved my mother—he spoke very quietly as he said this and looked down at the hospital sheets on his bed—he said that he was sorry she had gone through so much in the past two years. He was afraid that he had not been kind enough to her, and he mentioned a couple of occasions in their marriage when he had hurt her. But he knew that she loved him—and there was an expression on his recently weak face which can never be understood by a son.

He said that he had made a lot of money with the company so that we would never have to worry about much of anything in life. That was his way of saying that he loved *me*.

He laughed weakly once when reflecting on all of the "crazy relatives"—his way of loving *them*. And his laugh was carried on to Barb's children, his grandchildren. Inside, I felt the regret which Judy and I had expressed to each other, that we had not yet had a child for him to see.

Only once did he briefly cry—when he remembered his parents—and he reiterated his belief in an afterlife, knowing that "someday" he would be with them. We sat in silence for several minutes, neither of us wanting to face directly the reality of "someday."

After almost three hours of our mutual stream of consciousness, I got up to leave. Ironically, in the process of unmasking our lives to each other, I had had to wear a mask over most of my face, for he was in "isolation" from visitors' germs—and he couldn't see the gaping wordlessness of my mouth.

As I left his room, he smiled the smile I had known my whole life—the smile which absolved the spankings and the "bad times"—and he said, "You'll probably always be a rebel, won't you?" He must have seen my eyes crease in a smile above the mask, and I knew that his question had been a statement of support. I cried during the ride to mother's house, but the tears were for me.

On that Palm Sunday, he was lying comatose, surrounded by doctors. I screamed out suddenly, "Let him go—please let him go!"

They did.

The nurse told me later that his head had abruptly turned in my direction when I screamed. She thought that he had held on to life until I got there.

We sat in the funeral home for three days, as hundreds of people told me why they had loved him. Because *he* had loved *them*.

Many told me not to cry—but what else is there?

As his casket was lowered into that almost-spring ground, I perceived for maybe the first time in my life that there are perhaps four or five people in the entire world who ultimately care about me, who would be deeply affected by my life or death. Four or five. And one of them was being lowered into the ground!

The tears were for me.

In my stammering, hesitating speech to the Unitarians, I tried to convey some of those memories. It was probably a pointless, unfair thing to do to them, for they had certainly not expected such a personal catharsis when they came to the Fellowship this morning.

But I needed a fellowship, and they were kind enough to offer it—and perhaps that is the point of worship together.

The tears were for me.

April 13

A female client is mixed up with a faculty member, and I am angry as hell by the whole thing.

Use the body and then pass it on.

She's only a coed, so why not screw her as often as possible —tell her I'm a poor faculty member and "my wife doesn't understand me," and need to be loved like everyone else!

Maybe I'll give her an "A" if she's really good.

Who the hell do these guys think they are?

Sometimes I feel that I carry around too many secrets. I hear so much during those counseling hours, so many lurid affairs and complicated lives and outrageous stories about students, faculty, administrators, local citizens.

And then I hear rumors about Warner Montgomery, and I get angrier—I want to scream, "Okay, Athens, if you want to spread rumors about this guy, then let me tell you the *truth* about some of your other stellar citizens—about this one and this one and this one . . ."

But the clients speak in confidentiality—and I remain silent.

It's hard to keep quiet sometimes, though.

I ain't no angel either.

It's *still* hard to keep quiet.

April 19

The Board meeting tonight was a contrast to the lethargy of the past few months—it seemed that each member had a new idea for action.

Fred mentioned his efforts on getting a "poverty lawyer" for Athens; Judy Klare was pushing memberships in the new "Common Cause" organization; Jerry Adams described a rather involved plan for political lobbying in Columbus. I hope that something comes out of all the enthusiasm.

Because of the financial crunch, it was decided not to replace me on the staff if I leave in July. The Board is counting on the Methodist merger to bring Chuck McCullough to U.C.M. as a co-director. And it appears that Mike is going to stay on in one capacity or another.

May 8

I realized once more today what an *idiot* I can be as a parent. Peter hit Jenny for some unaccountable reason.

I went over to him, hit him on the butt, and yelled, "We don't *hit* people!"

When he cried with increasing decibels, I yelled, "And don't make so much *noise* around here!"

He must think that I am both a son of a bitch and a raving maniac.

The evidence is in.

May 12

Each week I receive the Sunday bulletin from the Church of the Messiah, the parish I worked in in Detroit. It is sent dutifully by Bob Christman, whose last name perfectly describes his character.

He cared for his father for years, and when the old man died, Bob moved his belongings into the parish house.

He acts as secretary for the parish.

From his salary at the auto plant, he gives huge amounts to the parish, for programs, vestments or whatever is needed. But whenever he gives money to the church, he always gives an equal amount to a social service organization, such as CORE or CARE or an open-housing group.

He loves people, especially children, and *he lets them know it!*

Once, while waiting for a bus, he was brutally hit in the face by a young black man, apparently for no reason. Bob's response: "I could certainly understand his anger—we have tortured the blacks for so many years—I was just a symbol for his anger—I hope he didn't hurt his hand . . ."

I shrink in comparison to the man.

I shall always think that he is a saint. In the true meaning of that word.

He would be embarrassed if he knew that I was writing these words about him.

May 17

Tonight I attended what was probably my last Board meeting—and the members are probably just as happy that I won't appear again. I let out with a catharsis of anger and guilt and frustration, and they were kind enough to let it happen.

I yelled that nothing has changed in the past two years— that I have accomplished nothing in terms of social change— the police and courts still do whatever they wish—the political landscape is barren—the Montgomery case is a vivid example of the academic bureaucracy—the students don't know which way to turn for leadership and understanding—the legislature has been aggressive and abusive in its response to the events of a year ago—U.C.M. is rapidly becoming immobilized— people know that they have no voice in their national government—to hell with all of it!

Judy Klare commented that "things have always been this way," and, although her words angered me even more, I must admit that she is probably right.

The others were rather silent, either because they could think of no response or because I came on like a locomotive.

It felt good to let it all out, but I feel badly about it now. I wasn't really yelling at those particular people, for they must certainly feel the same impotence as I.

I feel badly about it because they were so willing to listen to my ravings.

I tried to tell them that I love them for their concern and support, but it didn't come out very well.

I can't apologize for feeling all of these pressures—and I don't expect them to apologize for resenting my outburst.

Whom do I yell at, then?

May 21

During an interview at the Toledo Medical School this afternoon, I was impressed again by the length of time it will take me to get "certified" in medicine. My kids will probably be in their teens before I can hang out the shingle!

May 27

The cooperation from some of the doctors at the Health Center is a constantly reassuring and supportive aspect of our ministry. We would be literally lost without them, and I try to make that clear to them as often as possible.

But there is one doctor who is so consistently cruel and insensitive that Don and I felt we had to do *something*. We're both tired of hearing horror stories from crying coeds, stories that seem incredible but are verified by witnesses. We have tried to make our viewpoint known through Earl, but he gets nowhere either.

So Don and I had a meeting with a Cutler Hall administrator—and the bureaucracy chewed us up and spit us out. Perfectly.

"Gentlemen, I understand your concern, but nothing can be done by this office." he said with a smile.

"Why not?" we wanted to know.

"These cases are all a matter of the physician's judgment."

"You mean defaming young women because they are pregnant or because they ask for the pill is a matter of judgment?"

"Yes, it is. I may not agree with the doctor, but that's not the issue."

"What is the issue?"

"One issue is that it is *very* difficult to get staff physicians."

"Now I understand the issue," I said sardonically.

"Well, if you have some conclusive proof which a patient would want to pursue through the courts, then you have that option."

"But *you* aren't going to do anything, right?"

"There's nothing to be done at this time," he assured us.

"Will you at least *talk* with the doctor about the situation?"

"No, that's not my job."

"But we thought you were in charge!"

"Not in matters of a physician's judgment."

"Who is, then?"

"The physician."

Catch 22.

May 29

I received a rather delightful ecology message from the American Museum of Natural History a couple of weeks ago, so I decided to send it out in a newsletter.

I think that my numerous newsletters in the past few weeks reflect my anxiety about leaving this job. I know that I'm trying to flood the area with my views and hopes and frustrations. I'm afraid of losing my public voice, of losing what few credentials I have for speaking to this community. In some last, desperate attempt at social salvation, I'm beating people over the head with post-office homilies. I'm trying to jam the last few weeks with all of the issues and appeals and demands which nag at me constantly—and it's so obvious to everyone, I'm sure.

I nag and inwardly apologize in the same moment. Is that a sign of madness?

May 30

I can't understand the divorces—I mean I know some of the reasons involved, but I can't think of many antidotes. People seem to be simply growing apart—wanting different life-styles —opting for different hopes. And some couples try so hard to develop the "perfect" marriage that they end up with none at all . . .

I am working directly or indirectly with twelve couples at the moment, and I think that at least eleven had already decided to get a divorce before I saw them.

Don't let anyone ever tell you that "divorces are easy nowadays." I have never seen an "easy" one—there are too many historical facts and secrets in a marriage to make it easy to end. In terms of morale and guilt and legal processes, it's a hell of an experience for all involved. It is the only part of counseling that I really don't enjoy—because I feel so frustrated. That's *my* problem.

June 2

The Sociology Department made a bold move and offered Warner Montgomery a faculty appointment after the academic hearing upheld the decision of the College of Education to fire him. The new offer was made with the stipulation that the salary had to be raised outside of the department, for there is simply no money available within it.

Consequently, there was a rally yesterday to take financial pledges from individuals and to organize a fund-raising campaign in the dorms.

I talked with the student leader of the campaign this morning, and he says that they probably won't be able to raise more than half of the salary amount, even with the substantial private pledges.

Farewell, Warner.

June 4

Eric and K. B. Roth, whom I married last summer, have become dear friends of ours, and the four of us are planning a camping trip into Ontario in the next couple of weeks. I can't wait to get away!

June 6

At 6:55 this morning, I got the first word that Marie had been murdered.

Marie—grad student, artist, friend, counselee—a person who had let me hear the most intimate thoughts about her life —has been beaten to death in her bed.

My God, I've never had a day like this.

Talk with the police . . . and then talk some more.

Console the estranged husband . . . hold his head in my lap as he gets sick to his stomach . . . hear his words that I already know . . . that they had worked out so many of their problems. . . . "It can't end like this" . . . to know what he knows, that a husband is always a suspect . . .

Call the husband's family.

Accompany him to the terrible coldness of the morgue to identify the body . . . sick to my stomach . . . yes, that's her . . . the husband is collapsing onto the tile floor . . . will someone please help me . . . one officer out of many finally helps me support the husband . . . I can't get the scene out of my mind.

A long-distance call to Marie's father . . . I don't know

how to say this, sir, but Marie is dead . . . yes, it was a murder . . . I don't know . . . yes, please come as soon as possible . . . I cry and my hands shake as I hang up.

The husband is left at his apartment with his recently arrived family . . . let him rest awhile . . . give the car keys to the deputies so they can search it . . . go to the parking lot and point out his car . . . an officer says, "Once you have been involved with a murder case, you will never forget it" . . . I pray that he is wrong.

Meet Marie's family at my house . . . talk about her and how she should be buried . . . will I do the service . . . yes, I would be honored . . . but what do I say or do? I tell the mother not to view the body . . . remember Marie as she will . . . I wish that *I* could remember in a different way . . .

Don Bubenzer helps with much of it . . . God, I depend on him so much . . . our eyes meet occasionally, saying *what in the hell is going on* . . . why am I so weak that I tremble . . . I've seen death many times . . . but never *brutal* death . . . before my eyes, the results scream at me . . . but it still doesn't seem to be true . . . I want to vomit again, but I haven't eaten . . . I want to hold Judy and feel the warmth and comfort of her body . . . I feel so cold.

Help get the year-old baby from the county home . . . the baby I baptized . . . when was that . . . I don't remember . . . but it was happy and everyone was proud . . . the husband wants to hold the baby.

Earl calls . . . oh, Earl, what is going on . . . has this really happened . . . why can't I stop trembling, Earl . . . you're the psychiatrist . . . tell me what to do . . . this was going to be a quiet Sunday around the house . . . I don't know if I can handle this . . . how can I minister to the family when I can't keep myself together . . . I want to be strong . . . I really do . . .

June 7

It seemed that most of the front page of the *Messenger* was covered with the story of the murder, and there is no question that the paper is suggesting the guilt of the husband.

The sheriff said in the paper that the husband tried to impede the investigation by declining to have the car and apartment searched. That's *bullshit!* I was *there*—gave the keys to the police, watched them search it! "Sheriff Shields said (the husband) acted on the advice of the Rev. Thomas L. Jackson, campus minister, who had married the (couple)." Where did he get his *facts*—I told the husband to *help* the police and to get a lawyer if any charges were filed. A warrant was obtained and the apartment was searched, but they didn't even need a warrant for the car . . .

What are we going to have now—a kangaroo court or trial by newspaper?

June 8

In the midst of exam week, we held the Requiem Mass for Marie in the campus chapel at noon. Don and I tried to keep it light and hopeful, but there was little that we could say— everything is so ambiguous at this point. Both families were there, along with many others, and I shall never forget the pressure of this day.

Marie's younger sister is much like Marie—trying to be gentle and loving to all concerned. But the families are pretty much in a state of shock, as we all are.

Don helped me through the mass, and then stayed with me as I cried afterward. He said many of the words at the grave, thank God, and Marie was buried near a beautiful tree in

Athens, Ohio—this town which meant so much to her, which carried so many memories.

During the mass, I read the words from e. e. cummings which she loved: "I'd rather learn from one bird how to sing/ than to teach ten thousand stars how not to dance."

The *Messenger* printed my denial of yesterday's story regarding the search of the car, but I wonder who believes it. The sheriff thinks he has the murder weapon.

June 9

The front of the *Messenger* carried a story about the funeral, together with a large picture of the two families coming out of the chapel. The picture shows that the husband is black and Marie's sister is white—and now all of the readers can add that bit of information to the "evidence."

For the first time since our arrival in Athens, I have kept the doors locked at night.

The brutality of the murder and the hostility of the situation this week have finally gotten to me. I feel isolated from everyone but my family and a few friends. I want to escape, to withdraw. I don't have the strength to be everything to everybody.

And, absurdly, in the midst of all this, I have taken my two final exams. I don't remember what was on them.

June 12

I guess that the "murder weapon" turned out not to be the murder weapon, and the police seem to be baffled at this point. So am I.

Each of my courses resulted in an A—but that seems suddenly trivial.

As we prepare to leave on the camping trip, I have sent out a "farewell" newsletter from U.C.M., a newsletter I wrote last week before Marie was killed. It seemed almost embarrassing to send it out now, for it was filled with some personal notes of joy about the past couple of years. But these several harrowing days cannot—must not—deny the exultations of the past.

Again, we must celebrate when we can.

IX

Through the years, a man peoples a space with images of provinces, kingdoms, mountains, bays, ships, islands, fishes, rooms, tools, stars, horses, and people. Shortly before his death, he discovers that the patient labyrinth of lines traces the image of his own face.

—Jorge Luis Borges

September 15, 1971

A long summer of courses, decisions, and new directions. At the end of July, after considering the interviews at three medical schools, after realizing that the medical course would take me through at least eight years of separation from my family, I decided to change over to psychology. It will allow me to do the sorts of things I have in mind for my future, with perhaps only three or four more years of academic work. I hope that this is finally it.

I have been allowed to register in graduate psychology courses for this quarter, although I am not considered as a regular degree candidate—I will have to apply for that later. The competition is extremely strong, and I will simply have to wait and see.

So far, I have received A's in all of my courses, but that may change as I get into graduate work, especially in Statistics!

I have talked with Bill Choyke, the new editor of the *Post,* and he is willing to accept the possibility of a "weekly column" from my withered brain. I look forward to it.

A year ago today I was looking with eager anticipation toward a new year with a new staff at U.C.M. I wonder where in the hell I will be a year from now . . .

September 18

For our "going away present," U.C.M. has given us a surprise: a portrait of Judy and me, painted by Susan, the coed who lived with us last year! It is a beautiful thing—it shows the woman I love, it was done by a woman who has become a member of our family, and it was given by a group which gave me the freedom to do my own ministry. Although I feel the embarrassment of receiving a portrait of myself, I shall treasure the gift always. Another rubber monkey.

October 8

I become increasingly convinced that theology—"the study of the nature of God"—is an absurd activity.

To use the word "God" is to assume some basic, supreme "characteristics"—omniscience, omnipotence, omnipresence—faculties and powers beyond the human.

And beyond the human comprehension.

We take the idea of "God" and assign it the extensions of our own hopes, while we do not understand even the *finite* implications of our hopes.

I realize, of course, that our construct of God develops from our need to give life order and sense—but how dare we presume that what we have defined has anything to do at all with the reality of a "supreme being!"

The progression is undeviating: belief in God—definition of

God—recording of "Godly" activity—redefinition of God—
canonization of definitions of God—rules for understanding
God—sanctification of special group to *thoroughly* understand
God—more rules—exclusion of people who do not understand
God in the same symbols—deification of rules—buildings for
deposit of rules—and finally the equation of God with the
rules, the building, the select group, the definition.

Absurdly, we say that God:

> Loves us
> Tests us
> Judges us
> Tempts us
> Saves us
> Damns us
> Protects us
> Kills us
> Tricks us
> Illuminates us
> Tortures us
> Encourages us
> Humbles us
> Comforts us
> Challenges us

when, in fact, we don't know *any* of these things. We know
that these events and emotions exist in our lives, and our
desperation for order and sense compels us to make them the
activity of a supreme being—and in that very act, we limit the
unlimitedness of the Universal.

I don't know if God does these things, and I define "blas-
phemy" as my assumption that I would understand the activity
of God. Or Christ.

The only thing I can imagine as superior to the human
condition is a force of love-connection-acceptance, for it is

only that kind of force we seem unable to attain. We are competent at evil, as Camus' "Spitting Cell" testifies.

So when I do my own "blaspheming"—by attempting to define the Universal—I will opt for the force which loves and accepts beyond my comprehension.

I cannot define or limit beyond that.

It is enough to give me whatever "meaning" I need for existence. And it is too little to give me a reason for killing people who may believe differently.

October 10

This is the "honest" generation, right? From Woodstock (try to forget Altamont) to Athens, the press extols the virtues of a generation which is finally aware, sensitive, open, free, footloose, challenging, perceptive, unhypocritical—in a word, honest. Some of it seems true and nice and sincere, but a lot of it goes sour when we under-30s begin to believe too many press clippings about us, when we forget the sometimes astounding efforts at wholeness by our immediate ancestors, or when, as I would like to now suggest, we take a myth about ourselves and turn it into a fairly unrealistic fad.

I speak specifically of "honesty" as it relates to those most involved of human encounters, those things we call interpersonal relationships.

During the past two years especially, as I've tried to act as some sort of counselor for increasing numbers of couples who are having "difficulties," I have been struck by the mythology and unreality of much that goes under the title of "honesty." It is a conflict, I think, of a generation which has been guided morally by the Protestant ethic, post-Victorian sexual morés, and *Reader's Digest* success stories, while simultaneously searching for and believing the very antithesis of these things. It is really no one's fault, but there has not been time to consider the opposites, to distill the best from both, to find some real freedom in the stability of the immediate past.

And so?

So I notice more and more couples (whether legally married or trying cohabitation) are speaking in the *absolute* about their relationships: "Oh, Freddy and I have decided to be totally open and honest with each other . . . no secrets . . . no evasions . . . just always what we want . . . open . . . honest . . . really, no secrets."

And Freddy stands there, proudly nodding assent.

And I give them less than two weeks before the vigoro hits the fan or before an irreparable remark is made or before someone's "ultimate secret" lies throbbing "out on the table," defenseless and maybe a bit too much to handle.

I think of the guy who went home after work and told his wife (who was sweating over dinner and four kids) that he had just seen the most beautiful chick on the street. Honest with his sexual feelings.

I think of the attractive girl in the "sensitivity lab" who was literally terrified that she was ugly. Why? Because two guys in a car had yelled at her about how ugly she was. Another honest expression of personal feelings.

I think of the old political cliché that there is no one who can morally stand to have a private detective follow him twenty-four hours a day, because we all have our secrets. Great.

Why in hell can't each of us have our private world, our inner sanctum, our crazy little lands of fantasy and imagination, without having to always "come clean" to some other mortals, however loving, however accepting?

Why in hell is that concept so foreign to a generation which alternately demands freedom from government snooping, pleads for an end to constant depersonalization within society, and so often rejects that which is harmful and destructive?

There is a fine line there, that boundary between the cohesive and the destructive. There is much for two people to celebrate in their relationship, many things to do and enjoy and remember with fondness, countless things to speak and share and offer to one another. But, regardless of their "openness," those two people are still individuals, and that's sort of beautiful, too.

We all like to think that we're terribly liberated and totally accepting of others, and yet I think we sometimes risk our very worlds with those assumptions.

Maybe our kids will understand the whole thing better. Perhaps, like all other generations, we are simply caught between the old and the new, wondering what to do with the now.

November 4

I suppose that the best indication of the quietness, boredom, and apathy on campus this year can be found in the fact that most of this quarter has been dedicated to a discussion of Miss America.

Laurel Lee Schaefer, a recent graduate of Ohio University, was chosen as Miss America in the usual gauche "pageant" in September. Of course, the Alumni Association was thrilled with it all, but Miss Schaefer has made some rather silly and pathetic public statements on national radio and television, regarding her sexual innocence, her support of the present Vietnam strategy, and her genuine delight with the thoughts of Nixon and Agnew.

In one of my columns a few weeks ago, I tried to poke some fun at Miss Schaefer, and I didn't even mention that her rather casual comments about the war were being paid for by American and Vietnamese lives. On October 29, however, the "debate" escalated when the *Post* printed statements by some close acquaintances of Miss Schaefer which clearly questioned her "purity." These "revelations" were balanced by an editorial from the *Columbus Dispatch* which suggested that Miss Schaefer was the embodiment of everything we hold dear in this country.

So, the battle has waged ever since, with charges and countercharges about libel against the *Post*, and on and on. I grow tired of my own part in it . . .

With the war still raging both in Vietnam and in our nation's streets, we at Ohio University (the "seat of wisdom") spend a few months debating the comparative innocence and intelligence of Miss America. Hoo boy.

November 18

I have learned from a friend who is on the faculty that my application for admission to regular degree status in psychology may be considered more in political than academic terms. It seems that I am "the fellow who was involved in the rioting in '70" or something like that. I thought that sort of crap was finished!

The staff of the *Post* is still getting hassled over the Miss America thing, with plenty of threats of "censorship" from the Student Activities Board (S.A.B.). I wonder if the general student population could care less.

November 22

Something has been happening inside in the past couple of weeks. I find that anger is building up rapidly, but it seems to be that horrendous "general anger" which is aimed at no one and everyone. This quarter has left me somewhat depressed by its quietness, its lethargy, its smugness, its tremendous triviality.

Miss America was the issue on campus. Phases I and II overwhelm our minds. All of this while very little happens to change the war (the forty-thousand-foot-high bombers replace the footsoldiers, with even more efficient destructive power) or the mood of this nation (it seems that every American is in a different interest group, despising every other interest group). Yeah, my classes are going fine, but that is simply not enough. Something is eating away at me, at a lot of us.

Maybe, after all, it was the long talk Judy and I had the other night, when we realized that nothing has basically changed for the better in the past four years, and it ain't going to for quite awhile.

So why fight it any more?

Four years ago, when we had a parish in the ghetto in Detroit, we saw the area burn in frustration and anger—and things haven't changed at all since then, except that there are more rats now.

Our suburban-parish experience taught us that the gang with the money will call the shots every time, and if you question any improvement in that situation, simply check out any city you want to, including Athens.

The list could go on, but the point seems clear to us: the silent majority has won, and we are ready to admit it.

In the past four years, we have moved from a nation debating priorities to a nation sleeping. So maybe we just join in the slumber for awhile. We know where the power is and no one who's got it is going to give it up.

On one of the walls of our home hangs a quotation from William Sloane Coffin, and perhaps these words say much about our present viewpoint: *Hope arouses, as nothing else can arouse, a passion for the possible.*

We know that we cannot live without that hope, but our experience in the past few years would suggest "hope" and "the possible" may be found presently in the smaller, one-to-one efforts, rather than in efforts of wider scope.

After seeing too many friends get their asses kicked or appointed to do-nothing committees—and seeing ourselves spend too many hours debating issues that go nowhere—then it is time to back off a bit and try to do something on an "immediate" scale.

Hope arouses, as nothing else can arouse, a passion for the possible.

December 3

I sent out a "Christmas letter" to our friends; I tried to emphasize the relationship between all creatures on earth. I made it more positive than I really feel: no reason to depress others.

December 8

A letter arrives from Tom Niccolls:

> Your Christmas letter came and made me want to share it with many. How much meaning remains in the Nativity story and particularly when seen through your perceptive lines. Thank you for sharing your concerns.
>
> When thoughts turn to Athens—as they do from time to time—I always wonder and wish—hope and pray?—that your life there continues to be embraced with meaning and love. Are the studies for you what they were for me—both joy and frustration? I never could quite reconcile myself to the luxury of uninvolved scholarship—and from time to time when my Calvinistic conscience would ache too much, I'd pacify it with a foray into some action—however insignificant.
>
> Now the tables are turned. With (the building of my house) I get guilty feelings about not spending enough time on course

preparation. The ironies of life! We fluctuate between despair and hope that we'll ever have the house done . . .

I'm heading for the hospital tomorrow to have a lump removed from my right breast. Betty says, "Are you going through change of life?" There's a very small chance it's malignant, doc says, but we don't want to take chances. Gives a fellow an interesting perspective on life. As some brother said, "Now my lessons confront me."

Give hugs all around. And may the glad goodness of the Savior be with you.

Love,
Tom

December 28

Earl went to California in early fall to get some further training in psychiatry, and we didn't have a chance to say good-bye because of our brief trip to Canada. He felt that his marriage was over—we talked through hours and hours of that along with Jude. I miss him very much—the way we laughed over the absurdities—sometimes laughing nervously because the other emotions of life can be a bit too heavy to handle.

I called Earl tonight to say hello and wish him a Merry Christmas. I had never experienced him this low.

I told him that we loved him very much, but the conversation sort of petered out, and we both finally hung up.

January 3, 1972

My recent feelings of impotence and frustration were answered in today's mail. A letter arrived from an old friend, a guy who has been dean of a cathedral for some years, is unusually bright and perceptive . . . in short, a man I have respected as a genuine asset to the church. The letter informed me that he has left the cathedral in order to start his own consulting company, and he is very happy with his new life:

Vermont Royster in his holiday column in the Wall Street Journal asks whether faith in man is worth preserving. He comes to the conclusion, in a rather listless mood, that it is.

Poor Vermont, and all his poor compatriots; their celebrations of the Holy Day are nagged by fear, guilt, profound doubt and the very despair they lament in their brothers.

Their babel is the heritage of the Tower designed to make men as Gods.

A man is a man. God is God. Once this identity problem is straightened out, some of the other problems fall into place. Who promised, hinted, alluded or claimed man's immortality? Not God. Not Jesus.

Death at the end of my time is enough of history for me. I like to eat, sleep, make love, dance and defecate. The possibility of more than my senses projected into universal dimensions is too much for me to bear.

I will stretch to comprehend, to know, to grow, to take into me all that my eyes see, my ears hear, my nose smells, my tongue tastes, touches and feels; the lips of my beloved are sometimes more than enough of ecstasy.

But I will not seek the garden of repose, the peace that passeth understanding, because that's already been given, promised and assured in the very body I am. I can be myself. You can be yourself. We don't need to be nagged any more.

Jesus said, "God loves you *as you are*. That's the way He made you. That's the way He wants, accepts and loves you. All the others who've been telling you that you are no damn good, are liars, snakes, dogs, (bastards) so let them be consigned to their own damnation." "You, you who are children deep down, are free to be children and that's what the Kingdom of God is all about."

I have a suggestion for those of you who want to know what Christmas is all about. Walk out in the snow in your skivvies. Take up two handfulls and rub yourself clean with the snow. Then walk inside and hold close to you one child, man, woman, dog, cat, mouse or any other living creature bigger than a louse. Feel the warm. Lift a bottle of wine to your lips (or tea, hot chocolate, coffee) and feel the warm.

You're alive and well and in the land of the everliving love.

So what else, Old Royster Doyster, did you want?

Peter

So what else, old Jackson, did you want . . . or expect from life? Added to the letter was a penned note:

Thank you for your gift (to UNICEF) in our name. Nothing could please us more.

Glad to hear you are making alternative plans already rather than continuing frustrated in the church. It seems to be true, as the French worker priests found, that one can be a Christian or a Churchman, but not both.

We are thoroughly enjoying our new freedom. Peter comes home exhilerated every day—says the greatest thing is that the hostilities are out in the open and can be dealt with.

Glad to hear from you—
Mary and Peter

I don't really know how to respond. I don't know what I expect from humanity, from me. Too much, I'm sure. But what are the alternatives to all the garbage going on around us? If the hostilities are truly out in the open, *how* do we deal with them? *Mea culpa, mea culpa.*

January 22

A very surprising letter arrived today from the wife of a strongly militant student of two years ago:

Dear Tom:

I hope that you and your family are well. I'm sorry that I didn't write to you last year, but I have really been through some bummers. M. and I did finally split up, and it really put me through some changes. I finally quit my job teaching, lost about thirty pounds, and got into a very "exciting" life, so I thought, as a rock-n-roll star.

I went out to Boulder, Colorado and bummed around for nearly a year. I'm sorry that we never paid you back for giving M. the (moving expenses) loan. I had to pay $200 for his summer school, and then he split on me the next day . . .

Anyhow, I am writing to you because I have joined a revolution for Jesus Christ. I had run into "Jesus Freaks" before and really been turned off because it sounded like another trip. Most of the Jesus People really hate us (The Children of God) because we are too revolutionary. Anyhow, we have just opened up a new colony in Athens, and if our revolution grows as quickly as it has in the past year, I'm sure that you will hear about it.

All I can say is that we believe in the Bible, every word of it, cover to cover, book to book, chapter to chapter, verse to verse, word for word, and letter for letter. We live very similarly to the Early Apostles (Acts 2:44,45)

And we believe that America is about to fall apart, physically as well as spiritually, because she has worshipped materialism and forsaken God (Jer. 1:16).

We believe that God and his chosen prophets are directing this revolution because it has grown so quickly and because God speaks to us and gives us a vision of what and why it is happening. Two years ago we had four colonies; now we have close to a hundred colonies and 2000 disciples. None of us works for a living or have any visible source of income. We trust God to supply all of our needs, and he does. (Matthew 6:31–34).

I live in a colony at Woodland Park with about 100 disciples. We read and study the Bible for about 6 hours a day. Most of us were heavily into drugs at one time. Here, there is no smoking, no dope, no sex, no dating (we are permitted to get married, provided it is God's will). But I really dig it because I know this revolution will win. Eventually, all of us will become leaders of other colonies (Mark 16:15).

I felt that you would be interested in our revolution because I know how you felt about churches. Jesus' biggest enemies were the scribes and the pharisees. He told people to drop out and be communists (John 15:18,19 and Acts 4:34).

The differences between us and the Weathermen is that our revolution is based on love. We are a volunteer army, and we give up our materialistic possessions because we love Jesus (Luke 14:33 and Matthew 6:19–20).

I am enclosing some information about us and our "set card." We try to memorize at least one verse a day so that we will be able to witness boldly.

Do you remember "Adam" from "Bonanza"? He is one of our disciples. So is Jeremy Spencer from "Fleetwood Mack," an English rock group.

Anyhow, I hope that you and Judy run into the Children of God, because they are beautiful people. I have never been able to live with *anybody* (not even M.) and get along with them because I was so hung up on myself. This revolution allows you to completely give all of your love to Jesus, and because of the giving, dozens of people can live together, day in and day out, without arguments, contentions and bad feelings (I John 3:16).

I have written to M. several times to try to get him to check out the Children of God, because I think he would be a good revolutionary, because it's much easier to serve the Lord than it is to serve a doctrine made by men that are not in tune with God (Matt. 6:24).

You may have heard of our vigils throughout the country, where we put on sackcloth and ashes, and carry scrolls written from the Bible, with such messages as "The nation and kingdom that will not serve God shall perish." And we carry big staffs, which we bang in unison, and shout WOE at various intervals. One time we marched into a Jerry Rubin rally carrying a coffin. There were only 24 disciples, and they were silent except for their staffs coming down in a loud thump in unison as they marched in and for their periodic scream of WOE. But we completely stole the show, and the people there were all stunned into silence because they realized that *God was speaking*. In fact, Jerry Rubin talked with us for four hours, and he said that he would join our revolution if *his* failed.

I hope that you have time to write because I really love you and would like to hear how you and your family are doing. Sometimes it takes awhile for mail to get through, and I could be transferred to a new colony any minute. I love you people.

Love,
Ann

February 9

MAN:

1. An adult male human being. 2. A human being; a person. 3. Mankind. 4. A male human being having qualities considered characteristic of mankind. 5. A husband, lover, or sweetheart. 6. Any workman, servant, or subordinate. 7. Any of the pieces used in board games, as chess. (The American Heritage Dictionary)

So what is it?

What am I?

What am I supposed to be?

An adult/male/human/being/person/mankind/husband/lover/sweetheart/workman/servant . . .

Or part of a board game, as a pawn.

What are these qualities which are so characteristic of manhood?

Hairy? Strong? Brutal? Aggressive? Cynical? Militant? Surly? Hard?

Gentle? Compassionate? Accepting? Sincere? Passionate? Empathetic? Sympathetic?

My world tells me that mankind came to completion in the human person—the man—of Jesus. I am told that this is the ultimate in personhood, whatever he was. I am told that this is the model.

But the models which are forced upon me from every direction are the John Wayne—Curtis LeMay—J. Edgar Hoover —Spiro Agnew—Charles Atlas—S. I. Hayakawa—Billy Graham—Eric Hoffer—John Mitchell personalities. But the clay feet crumble, while the models fail to realize that they are footless.

So what model do I offer to my own son?

I know now.

I'll tell him about Uncle Harry, who never made a lot of money (the ultimate judgment of our society), but whose face and hands show the lines of gentleness and warmth and unassuming strength. I will take Peter to Harry, and say, "That's what it is about."

I'll tell him about Charlie Ewing, the black fellow who always comes with us to paint and fix the next house in our travels. I will take Peter to Charlie, and say, "Listen to his laugh."

And I'll take him to Tom/Don/Fred/Harry/Edgar/Davis/Bob/Earl/Eric/Geoff and a score of other unnamed lives so that he will know that a *man* is one who tries not to kill but to create.

March 15

There has not been much to write about in the past few weeks, but I have been trying to solidify some options for next year.

I have entered applications at four schools of graduate psychology to pursue the doctoral program. As another option, I have applied to three graduate schools of hospital administration, for it seems like something I could grow to enjoy—it attracts the "generalist" in me.

Although I continue to feel much of the lethargy which has overcome the nation—even the lack of excitement or anticipation of the political campaigns—I am feeling less anxious, almost stoic about much that is going on—or not going on. I don't mean that in a negative way, for I feel much less of the weight of the world on my shoulders.

I know that my head is helped appreciably by my growing relationship with Eric Roth, who is in charge of a "group home" for juvenile offenders in Columbus. He is a different personality from anyone I have ever met before, with an easygoing sense of enjoyment of this bizarre world; his ability to laugh at the absurd is sometimes thankfully infectious to my own soul.

Eric is about six foot four, fluctuates between two and three hundred pounds, has an active and intuitive mind, continually inhabits a flannel lumberman's shirt, and is disarmingly unaffected from his full red beard to his immense shoes.

He grew up in the street contest known as the Bronx; he hustled pool for a couple of years to make money for college; at O.U., he and some friends joined a dying fraternity only to have a house for themselves; he is irreverent on almost any subject, but shares our concerns about so much.

Mainly though, as some Ken Kesey hero would do, he is able to confront the world head on—and then laugh *at* it or *with* it, whichever it deserves.

That is a gift. He helps me laugh.

But I am me.

April 8

It all seemed to come together in my head a few days ago —in a theater in Denver.

I had been accepted into the hospital-administration program at the University of Colorado Medical School in Denver, and I suddenly decided to fly there to look over the school and the housing situation.

The houses were nice, the school was magnificent, the staff was superb—and right in the middle of a group discussion with some faculty, I knew that I was kidding myself about the whole thing.

I went back to the Holiday Inn and stared at my room walls for a couple of hours.

In the middle of Denver, Colorado. Alone. Knowing what I *didn't* want to do, but that was all.

I had to get out for awhile, so I headed for a showing of *The Godfather* at a suburban theater at two in the afternoon. There were only a few other customers at that hour, and I sat in isolation on the left side of the theater.

As the story unfolded, all I could see was the relationship between this father and his sons; it mattered not what they were doing in the story itself—what *I* saw was the relationship. Suddenly I realized that this day was one day away from the anniversary of my own father's death—and then the screen forced me into deeper memories and terrible loneliness.

Why isn't he here to counsel me on my life?

Why did he have to die at fifty-three?

I left the theater after a deep, cleansing cry, returned to the walls of my room, and continued to stare.

I have to talk with someone.

I called Los Angeles for Bob Iles, a close friend from seminary days.

"Bob, I'm in Denver, my head's strung out, and I need to talk—and I thought you'd listen to me."

"I'll meet you at the airport."

We talked for three days—the good, the bad, the indifferent. He listened to three years of stream of consciousness, and I listened to his own battles won and lost in L.A. He put me in touch with grad schools, he showed me good areas to live in, he helped me sort out a few sections of the maze I've been running. It was good.

I did not feign the enthusiasm of my call to Jude. She could tell the excitement in my voice—that even if I am still uncertain about a lot of things, at least I have a *place* that looks possible and inviting.

Who in the hell would want to move to Los Angeles?

I do.

Why:

I dunno.

But there's all that *smog!*
I know.
You're crazy.
Yup.

X

Paradoxes are the only truths . . . Life is a constant
becoming: all stages lead to the beginning of others.

—George Bernard Shaw

June 21, 1972

We are packing the Ford station wagon again, this time
headed for Los Angeles.

We are beckoned by the land of sun and smog and Yorty and
Mickey Mouse . . . but mainly by the prospects of vocational
training.

I have been accepted into two different Ph.D. programs: one
in Urban Affairs at Southern Cal. and the other in Clinical
Psychology at the California School of Professional Psychology
(Los Angeles).

Which I will finally choose—and why exactly I am going—
seem patently unclear to me at this moment, but . . . what
the hell.

What is there to say of these past few years . . . these
times of turmoil and fellowship and confusion and closeness in
Athens and Jersey and Detroit? Shall I offer a few unnotable
paragraphs of pop theology or philosophical discourse to draw
together the insipid and the ingenious aspects of life and death?
No. No, for the opposites go in great circles and meet and
separate again in my mind, and I am left to only present a

210

series of conditions which exist at this very moment . . . and the reader is left to make the judgments of these lives and times:

* * *

On May 8, Richard Nixon announced *another* "final" solution to the Vietnamese conflict: the mining of harbors and the increased bombing of cities. The oddsmakers in Las Vegas tell us that Richard Nixon will be giving his second inaugural address next January.

* * *

Hundreds of students went into the streets again to protest the Vietnam policy: seventy-seven were arrested for a nonviolent sit-in. Judge Sheeter set bond at one thousand dollars per person.

* * *

The new mayor of Athens, a retired air force man who takes his job seriously, responded to student protests as a human being, without clubs or gas.

* * *

Several people were shot recently in a shopping center in North Carolina.

* * *

The old airport land, once discussed as a large park for area residents, is now going to become a huge hotel/shopping center site, across the street from the present large shopping center.

* * *

Fred Mong's desire to become a lawyer was not simply a fantasy: he put 35,000 miles on his car this year, commuting three times each week between Athens and a law school in Pittsburgh.

* * *

There is a new community swimming pool in Athens.

* * *

The crisis center was finally established, and numerous volunteers continue to take calls from people who need to communicate with another human being.

* * *

Tom Niccolls just finished building a huge house *himself* in Hiram.

* * *

The pastor of the First Methodist Church in Athens recently moved into a $70,000 home, paid for by the parish.

*   *   *

Angela Davis has been found not guilty of all charges.

*   *   *

The fellow who replaced me in New Jersey was told that there was not enough space in the $120,000 budget to pay his salary; he has become a campus minister.

*   *   *

Culver is now admitting female students, and the anachronism diminishes.

*   *   *

Don Bubenzer has resigned from U.C.M., and sees some new options in his graduate program in counseling.

*   *   *

John Kirkendall returned from Canada, turned himself into the naval authorities, and served some time in the brig before receiving a discharge. The last I heard, he had joined a religious community in Virginia.

*   *   *

Faculty sabbatical leaves have been canceled in all state universities for next year, in order to "conserve funds."

*   *   *

The university athletic department received another million-dollar budget.

*   *   *

A couple thousand Episcopal clergy are having trouble finding jobs.

*   *   *

The Athens County Children's Home was finally completed a few months ago, after two years of committee meetings.

*   *   *

Several of the "militants" from the spring of '70 have returned to school to enroll in premedical and paramedical programs; they hope to start a "medical collective" someday.

*   *   *

The *elected* Congress of the United States of America has not been consulted on the escalation of the war.

* * *

Don Craig is now the assistant to the vice-president for Educational Services at O.U.

* * *

The cafeteria where the "town leaders" used to meet each morning was destroyed by fire a few months ago.

* * *

Warner Montgomery is teaching in a predominately black college in South Carolina.

* * *

The College of Education lost some of its graduate accreditation, and the dean has resigned.

* * *

Lew Kemmerle, the former pastor of the Presbyterian parish, is teaching English at the university.

* * *

The murder of Marie is still unresolved.

* * *

Eric and K. B. Roth visit us almost every weekend from Columbus, bringing us more stories from the ghetto there.

* * *

A new police chief will be named within the next few months, and Capt. Charles Cochran is one of the candidates.

* * *

Another presidential candidate, George Wallace, has been shot; his apparent assailant is charged under the Civil Rights Act of 1968.

* * *

Judge Franklin Sheeter is running for the common-pleas bench in the fall election.

* * *

There are strong indications that U.C.M. will be down to a one-man staff within the next two years.

* * *

A housewife from Massachusetts has spent $15,000 of her own money to place full-page ads in Ohio newspapers—simply to ask citizens to write letters to Nixon about ending the war.

*   *   *

Various Church organizations have announced pending theological and liturgical changes in order to lure absent members.

*   *   *

After years of part-time academic endeavors—while raising three children and me—beautiful Jude has received her undergraduate degree . . . *cum laude*.

*   *   *

Jenny announced at dinner that she wants to be a nurse when she grows up; Peter said that he wants to be a mailbox.

*   *   *

A few weeks ago, Earl, my friend and confidant, died suddenly. It was a profound shock. I offered the following words to his children during the memorial service in the campus chapel:

> I would like to say just a few things to you about your father. I want you to know first, though, that I am a limited man, not only in terms of the words which I can think to say, but also because my emotional ties with your father were—and are—very strong and deep. I have tried for the last three days to find appropriate quotations from books—quotations which would say better than I can the beauty and sincerity and confusion and hope and uncertainty and love which were your father's life. But I was unsuccessful in my search—although the books described parts of Earl's life, yet his *exact* life—its uniqueness and power—was not to be found in any of them.
>
> So that is why I want to say these few words to you this afternoon. Today, tomorrow, this week, next month, next year, twenty years from now, as you remember your personal relationship with him, as you search for the many things which tied your various lives together, do not search through written words on a page in some book, but rather search through the people who stand and sit in this room and in rooms in all parts of the country, for *we* are the ones whom Earl helped, *we* are the ones with whom he laughed and cried and argued and celebrated and questioned and wondered . . . wondered about the amazing forces in life which

cause us all to do what we do. There are people in this room—and many others in different places—who can tell you how much he helped the direction of their lives, how he enabled them to sort out the positive and the negative, how he tried to give them a little better look at the freedom which was theirs to possess. That is why we are crying this week, that is why we are lamenting this day—for our tears are for ourselves, for our good memories, for our realization that we will miss him very much.

I say one more thing to both of you. There was never any doubt—and, to me, there is no doubt now—that your father loved you deeply and totally. If there were times when he imperfectly expressed that love—when he failed to say the right word at the right time—it was not because of lack of feeling. You both were in his thoughts constantly, and there were dozens of occasions when he told me, when he told you, when he told many others here how very proud and satisfied he was to have you as his children. There *are* times when we fathers forget—or seem unable—to say those things to our children directly, and we must ask for your forgiveness at such times.

I celebrate your father's life—and, like King David and Zorba, I shall dance in my own way. I hope that there will be times when we can all talk with you more about him, for there is much to say. Let's do that.

Amen.

*   *   *

I do not plan to renounce my priestly vows.

*   *   *

Edgar Whan told me the other day that moving to L.A. was simply a matter of "switching fleas," that I'll be scratching there too. Probably. I hope so, actually. Something's going to happen for us out there—or we'll make it happen!

XI

If, after all, men cannot always make history have a meaning, they can always act so that their own lives have one.

—Albert Camus,
Resistance, Rebellion, and Death

August 1, 1972

What's happening?

Why are these crazy thoughts and ideas coming into my skull?

Is it the too-hot rays of the Los Angeles sun—or the incessant painting and fixing of the house over the past six weeks—or the effect of swimming-pool chlorine on a Midwestern soul—or the sudden fragrance of trees and bushes and flowers on normally air-conditioned nostrils—or is it all the result of considering the past eight years, of remembering the begging and the turmoil and the hostilities and the nowhere results of efforts and risks and hopes?

No, it's more than that. So many of those things were negative and the memories are so bittersweet.

No, this is a surge I feel building within me, carrying me, demanding me to think in new ways, in new directions, in new means . . . but I can't get it straight, I don't know what exactly I'm feeling or thinking.

I dare not identify it today, for I might describe the wrong thing even to myself. I want to *change* something, I want to get ahold of something new and vibrant and hopeful and possible . . . and crazy?

August 3

I have a major hint as to the state of my mind; it is in the words of a letter I received a couple of weeks ago from an old seminary friend, a young priest who ministers in a small Texas town. Parts of the letter have been nagging at my gut with regularity:

> Your letter (about your move to Los Angeles) came while I was in Mexico so I am not very prompt in answering it (but Jesus forgives me anyway).
> How come you get to do all the neat stuff?
> I get stranger and stranger, curioser and curioser . . .
> My main interest in life right now seems to be making adobe bricks and golden eagles (I mean watching them—nobody but eagles make eagles).
> I may over the next three or so years:
> 1. Start a commune.
> 2. Start a retreat colony for fired clergy and families.
> 3. Build an adobe house.
> 4. Screw up and become a Cardinal-Rector type (or as close as I can come to that).
> What are you going to do with a Ph.D.?
> You can't build a house out of them. Or eat one.
> What are you going to do with all that stuff you are going to study?
> All those people in cities look alike to me. I think they would look alike to each other if they ever looked at each other. Us country people are different. We all look different to each other. We sure look different to most city folk!
> I may have to figure out some seminar in L.A. so I can see your house.
>
> Love,
> Hugh

So, Jackson, what's *your* major interest in life right now? What *are* you going to do with that Ph.D.? Build something with it? Eat it?

What *are* you going to do with all that "stuff" you're going to "study"?

Have you *truly* looked at all those city people . . . including yourself?

I want to look, I want to find out what is going on inside my brain and soul these past several days, I want to know what has meaning for my life . . . but how many questions can I ask myself, and how many answers can I give?

August 4

Could I risk the possibility of becoming a full-time writer? But what if I failed at it? Not materially or financially failed . . . but failed to write well. And what would I do with myself when I wasn't writing? An atrophied soul would emerge!

August 14

Is it totally predictable that the clarifying thought came to me as I walked through *Disneyland?*

Was it the Alice in Wonderland ride . . . or the twirling tea cups . . . or the final jolt of the Matterhorn cascade that firmed—or ultimately loosened—my frazzled brain?

Hesitatingly at first—and then with mounting enthusiasm —I mentioned the idea to Jude as we drove back from Anaheim.

"You know, woman, we've tried to accomplish so damned many things over the past several years . . . stop the war, change peoples' minds, quiet down racism, protect peoples' rights, listen to problems . . . you remember all that?

"Yeah, I remember all that."

"You want to know something interesting about all that?"

"I already know it: we didn't get too far with a lot of it!" And she still managed to smile in recollection.

"No, no. I mean, sure, we didn't get too damned far, but the interesting thing is that we always tried with someone else's *permission* . . ."

"What?"

"Really! We were always *begging* people to do something, always *pleading* with them to answer the inequities of society. Like *idiots,* we tried to save the world—which is pretty crazy in itself—but we always politely asked someone's *permission* to do *anything!*"

"And?" I think she was steeling herself for the reply.

"And I have an outrageous, insane, possibly workable plan."

"A plan for what?" She seemed to wince at the car ashtray.

"A plan to concentrate our efforts on a small chunk of the world."

"Which small chunk . . . I thought you were starting grad school next month."

"Listen to this. We set up a two-pronged effort. First, we find a business which has a good cash flow." She started to look incredulous when I mentioned the word business, but I continued. "You know, some business that doesn't rip people off. Second, we set up a private, charitable foundation. Are you with me so far?"

"Go on."

"Then we take most of the profits—hopefully—from the business, and shoot them into the foundation, and direct the foundation toward the real problems of the city . . . work with people who are always getting ignored by everyone else."

She thought for a few minutes and then, "You know, it really sounds like it could work, but it must be more complicated than that."

"Well, sure it's more complicated, but dammit, we could sink or swim without having to ask someone which stroke we can use. We could borrow some money from the estate to get started . . . we could *use* some of the money that Dad worked for . . . we could use it for something he would believe in . . ."

As I said each word, I seemed to find added enthusiasm for the next and the next and the next. I frequently looked at Jude's eyes, and I began to see that recognition of possibility which I feel inside myself. I knew that she was totally surprised by the suggestion, yet immediately caught by its craziness.

Tonight, the passion for the possible brews within each of us, with the joy and scariness of decision making.

August 18

Today I looked deeply at one of those city people.

Lloyd Wilson is a thirty-seven-year-old carpenter who has been working with me all summer on the house. He is one of the finest craftsmen I have ever personally encountered, and he exudes an interest in other people which is obvious upon first meeting.

During the frequent coffee breaks from our work, we have increasingly shared parts of our background, reminisced on similar experiences and learnings. Having been introduced by Bob Iles, one of my seminary classmates, we have come to some mutual understandings of how we are similar and yet different. His honesty about his own life has allowed me to reflect on mine.

You see, Lloyd is a "dry" alcoholic. In the past seven years, he has been through some of the crevices of hell, including the surreptitious drinking, the guilt involved in squandered money, the dishonesty in facing friends and family, the prolonged deceit of unreal cures, the catastrophe of a final breakdown, the initial humiliation and confusion of the state hospital, the wracking journey toward realization of self-worth . . .

But he made it, and he can now like himself.

What an incredible person that is in this present world: to know where he has been, to remember the expense, and to face the present with no apologies. The present. He lives in the now, knowing that it is better than what was . . . and a good taste of what can be.

Why do I mention all of this? To say that my own trepidation over my present thoughts demands a listener who has experienced so much . . . and is willing to *feel* my uncertainty and hope.

So I shared my idea with Lloyd during a long talk . . . and his eyes and his words told me that it is worth a try!

August 20

My thoughts go to dizzying heights about the possibilities of the venture, and I must constantly bring myself back to reality. But nothing is real yet about the whole thing.

Well, *one* thing is real: I drafted a letter to the graduate school to resign from the Ph.D. program . . . and my palms were sweating as I signed it.

I've spent hours searching the "Business Opportunities" column of the *Los Angeles Times*, trying to find three or four reasonable options. The earthworm distributorship (honest to God!) didn't sound too good.

I have gone around to several business brokers to see what they have to offer. Everything.

One broker was talking to me about convalescent hospitals: she told me that I could probably feed each patient on a buck a day . . . and make lots of bucks. I wanted to vomit.

August 21

I spent all day looking at car washes.

Car washes!

Would you believe it. These gigantic car washes wash a *lot* of cars—and they don't really seem to rip people off— what the hell, no one *has* to have his car washed, like he has to buy food or go to the hospital or buy shoes for the kid or whatever.

Why not?

We could even use the place for some employment for people who can't get jobs!

A car wash.

So I told Jude. She thought it was crazy enough.

So I told Lloyd. He said, "Why not?"

So I called Eric and told him: he laughed a lot and said, "What the hell, sounds good."

One problem: I will need a hell of a lot of money for the down payment, and I wonder if I truly have the guts to try for the money from my family. What can I tell them beyond what I dream?

August 27

I am back from a quick plane trip to Detroit and Athens, and the events seem more outrageous with each passing day, with each part of the dream.

After some lengthy discussion, my family in Michigan seemed to think that it was worth a try . . . and I have been given enough money for the initial cost.

They, in their benevolence, seem to trust me more than I do.

The basic insanity of the whole situation hit me during the trip back. I know almost nothing about the business world and, in fact, have never wanted to be a part of it.

Is it possible not to rip people off—to give them a basic service which they are looking for—and still make enough money to fund a reasonable foundation?

I will need some real help—would Lloyd be willing? What if he doesn't want to?

Anyway, the overnight stop in Athens reminded me of many things in the immediate past, and I realized how much has changed in these few short months. Even with seeing the beautiful faces which I have missed so much, I know that I am fundamentally pleased with this new direction.

October 15

So much has happened—I have had no time to record thoughts and feelings. Getting a bright young lawyer Steve Miller, finding a young, aggressive accountant, going through the escrow proceedings, listening to so many terms and jargony phrases which mean so little to me, experiencing the chaos of the two-week trial period—all of it churns around and through me in waves of hesitation and certainty. I have tentatively hired Lloyd as a "consultant"—he was in the insurance/business worlds before going back to carpentry three years ago—and he is capable of understanding all that is going on . . . and then explaining it to me.

We take over "officially" tomorrow, and we are eager for the chance to try things "our" way, whatever that means in success or failure.

I wonder what my seminary profs and my bishop and my friends of yesterday would think about this "priest in the car wash" stuff!

October 21

There are about twenty-three workers—five Mexican-Americans and the remainder black. I enjoy being with them, even though I can't communicate very well with the Chicanos, and I have briefly explained to the black workers that I am a priest, trying to make enough money to fund a community foundation. Strange looks and accepting smiles.

I decided to "work the line" with the Chicanos this afternoon, trying to discover the rhythm of wiping off cars, changing towels, and preventing backache. During a short respite between Eldorados, Mark IV's, and souped-up Volkswagens, I quickly mentioned that I was a *padre,* a revelation which brought amazing glances and a flurry of unknown words. Within sixty seconds of this announcement, I was wiping off the mammoth hood of a Toronado, and carelessly brought my right foot down in the path of the right front tire. As the car passed over my tennis-shoed foot, I let out a string of "worldly" epithets which would have melted steel . . . and the Chicanos cupped hands over mouths and muttered, "Oh padre . . . oh *padre!"* For the rest of the afternoon, they have called me *padre,* while coyly winking in some pact of mutual secrecy!

I now carry the "black badge of courage"—a wide tread mark on my tennis shoe—to remind me of my baptism into the world of car wash, hot wax, employee relations, gasoline fill-ups, and balance sheets . . .

November 8

It is amazing how little I have listened to national and world affairs in the past two months, and yet now—probably for only a few hours—the impact of the election has hit me. I knew that Nixon was going to win big, and I have faced the realization of living with him for the next four years. And I suppose that I can easily do that.

What staggers me, though, is the fact that by 1976, Richard Milhous Nixon will have been the major, consistent, political force in my *entire* adult life. Out of a nation of two hundred *million* people, this man has been chosen to make more decisions and to wield more power than any other human being in the last twenty-four years.

I don't know what that means or what that says about our nation, but I have a few hints. . . . We get what we deserve or pay for.

November 28

On February 3, 1971, I wrote a few lines about my relationship with Tom Niccolls: "I wonder if I will ever again work with someone who understands my thoughts almost before I think them, or with whom my personality and hopes and quirks mesh so well."

I now know the answer to that urgent question, for the uniqueness of Lloyd Wilson gives me the freedom to consider the possibilities of this odd existence. There is a strange telepathy which brings decisions into the open, an empathy which allows discussion, a sympathy which shares the ordeals of trying to fit a crazy scheme into a concrete world.

We have just experienced the worst month in several years in the car-wash business. Rain, cloudiness, few customers. My spirits seem to skyrocket or crash depending on the relative mood of the local weatherman. "Consider the lilies of the field," I once blared from the pulpit . . . but the helpful and faithful simile vanishes as I envy the lily for the growth it *gains* from the rain.

I am rescued, though, by the faith of others, and I remember Niccolls' words: "Now my lessons confront me."

I am rescued by the importance of Jude's accepting glances and perceptive questions and warm touch.

I am rescued by Lloyd's quiet humor after four days of rain: "Well, if we fail at this business, we can always go somewhere and start a campus ministry!"

I am rescued by friends—Wendy, Bob, Eric, Karol, the Athens crowd, my family—who accept not only the romance of the foundation idea, but also the struggle and demands of the business.

I am rescued. Is there a more important or more telling sentence than that?

December 17

I have come to realize that "ministry" in this world is not a matter of ordination or white round collars or geographic location—it is the confrontation of people who need each other.

Even as I try to think of ways to lure car-wash customers, I receive an urgent call from someone who knew me in New Jersey; telling me that her beautiful, talented niece is overdosing in a small apartment in Hollywood.

Even as I place a newspaper ad offering "free hot wax" for next Monday, I face the issue of one of my black employees who sits in jail on a purse-snatching charge, with no witness or evidence against him, with no collateral for the thousand-dollar bail, with no option but to sit for a few weeks until the charge is finally thrown out of court.

Even as I place a call to have some electrical equipment repaired, I realize that our home is now occupied by three nonfamily members who share our lives: an eighteen-year-old black fellow from our parish in Detroit who is enrolled in a paramedical program here; a twenty-three-year-old woman from Athens who is working hard at a department store job and a decision on her vocation; and a seventeen-year-old girl from Oklahoma who is trying to find a new life here, after burying her mother last spring and feeling now that her father wants nothing more to do with her. And I hear that another young black fellow is arriving in a week or so from Detroit, to stay with us for awhile until he finds work.

It all seems so complicated and demanding, and yet I love the diversity of it all, to know that family has not only the definition of "a group of persons related by blood or marriage," but also "a group or category of like things, as related organisms."

To know *both* definitions is to stay in touch with the joys and possibilities of "ministry."

December 19

Business has been terrible for the past several weeks, and I have had to pump more money into it to keep things going. Veterans in this business say that they haven't seen weather this consistently bad in fifteen or twenty years.

What the hell, a year ago I was crying in my own beer because nothing was happening with anything. Now, at least, we've stuck our necks out for a possibility, as weird as it is. And that seems better to *me* right now than sitting in a classroom taking notes.

Sometimes, when I'm alone in a room and it's very quiet, I get very scared about those promissory notes I signed for this business . . . and I worry about going broke . . . and I think of all the work ahead of us in trying to get the foundation going.

When I'm in that quiet room alone—and I know that I have to eventually leave it—I remind myself that in a hundred years it won't make any difference anyway.

There's only now—and the passion for the possible.

December 24

It is the eve of birth . . . not only of the Child, but of the particular hopes we have for our tiny corner of existence.

So much has happened . . . and so much can happen.

In the past couple days, business has increased by what seems to be a million percent . . . but that too could be fleeting.

A few days ago, I entered a bid for another car wash, one located only a few miles from here. One which could bring even more financial help to the foundation. Or financial disaster.

I have asked our lawyer to form the foundation as soon as possible, to name it "The Marcliff Foundation," in honor of my parents; for one who left us the resources to do all of this, and for one who continues to give us the courage to act.

In two days, Jude and I fly to Michigan for a reunion with many of our friends from Detroit and New Jersey and Athens. It will give us a chance to discuss further our plans here . . . to see if Eric and K. B. will move out here to help us with the foundation . . . to describe our present life to those who have known us previously.

Three days ago, I decided to make public our intent and reason for being at this present effort, and consequently published the following full-page ad in the local paper:

ARE WE CRAZY?

Paxco, Inc., is a new corporation, started by an Episcopal priest, dedicated to helping the community thru a private business enterprise.

Paxco, Inc., is the new owner of this car wash.

The idea is to put a substantial part of the business profits into a charitable foundation, so that the foundation can meet some of the desperate needs of the community:

—Like halfway houses for young people who need help or guidance.

—Like rehabilitation programs for people who have never had a real chance in life.

—Like other community programs which might allow your fellow citizens or yourself to live a more positive existence.

—Like trying to help people without regard to their color or their religious creed or their nationality . . . just PEOPLE.

All of this is based on the belief that a community business can provide enough income for a nonprofit foundation to help that same community.

Some people in the business world have told us that we are "crazy" to try such a thing.

They say that we will never "make it."

We will make it, if you will help us.

We are:

—lowering car wash prices.

—giving double Blue Chip Stamps on "Hot Wax."

—starting "Small Car Days" for extra savings on Tuesdays and Thursdays.

—improving wages and working conditions for our workers.

—improving the service for you!

Now, we need your new or continued support.

Are we "crazy" to try to help the community?

Your response will give us the answer.

We hope that you will want to do your business with a company which responds to your community.

Please tell your friends and neighbors about this . . . and we will keep you informed about our community plans.

"Paxco" means "peace company."

Peace.

We probably *are* crazy . . . but in a crazy world it somehow adds up to sanity to mix "hot wax" and "small-car days"

with halfway houses and ex-cons and community develop-
ment. In a world gone mad with killing and personal violence,
it seems to make sense to find the passion for the possible in
one's immediate surroundings.

Tonight, in the warmth and quietness of our candlelit living
room, I celebrated a Christmas Eve Mass with a few people
who are very dear to me. I silently prayed for forgiveness for
the rain of destruction which our American bombers are in-
flicting on North Vietnam this week, and I knew as I whispered
those words that I am powerless to stop *that* carnage.

But I am *not* powerless.

I do *not* have to give in totally to the insanity.

I have hands . . . and a brain . . . and some senses . . .
and some deep hopes for the first time in several years.

My "cathedral" is a car wash!

I am a clown in a circus world!

The rubber monkey is my proof!

Dammit, *we are going to make it!*

XII

To Be Is To Do
—Fromm
To Do Is To Be
—Nietzsche
Do Be Do Be Do
—Sinatra

—graffiti scrawled in men's room of a Hollywood bar

January 6, 1974

The real estate agent and I had logged a lot of miles driving around Ithaca, New York, looking at scores of expensive houses and farms. Obviously, he was startled when I finally decided upon a large, barnlike structure which sits next to a cascading waterfall. Over the past hundred years, the building has been variously used as a barn, a factory, a tannery, a house, and a duplex apartment.

"It'll take you *months* of full-time work to make that place into something," the agent offered, with a kindly wince.

"I know," I said. "That's the point."

October 5, 1973

Dear Lloyd, Steve, Mom, and Barb;

It is the early hours of Friday morning, and I can't seem to get sleepy with the various and considerable matters which are on my mind at this point. It would probably be a monumental

waste of time to reconsider the incidental events of this past
year, but they do roll around the sides of my gut and brain
with regularity. Broadly viewed, though, this year has pre-
sented the business with certain obstacles which increasingly
seem insurmountable. There has been the worst weather (rain
all *winter, no sun this summer), the flop of the economy, the*
record-setting inflationary spiral, the chaos of Watergate, the
cuts in gasoline allotments, the dramatic increase in utility
rates, the demoralized consumer, and other, more minor dis-
asters . . .

I spent much of the year watching people change. Myself
included. The vibrations of a corrupt government radiated a
mood of distrust, cynicism, and, in too many lives, despair. I
met thousands of people, and too often the comments reflected
the awareness of a country, an economy, a morale gone adrift.

As prices skyrocketed and unemployment put the poorest
again on the streets, I could feel the anxiety growing around
me and within me. Even as I tried to think of better advertisements to lure new customers, I increasingly realized that our
nonessential industry was just that: it's a hell of a lot more
important to put food on the table than to gas/wash/hot wax
the car—even in California's autopia.

I learned that business is business, that power is simply and
always a matter of supply and demand. With each passing
week, the omnipotence of the oil companies became more
obvious. All of us, whether dealers or consumers, unwittingly
increased our allegiance to that sovereign: the independents
went out of business, and prices/profits soared.

(October 5)
. . . We coincidentally took over the businesses just as the
crap hit the fan. It seemed logical to assume that business
would eventually improve, that we would gain reasonable

*profits. Simply put, business did not improve, and I'm con-
vinced that things will not get better in the foreseeable future.
And don't expect divine intervention!*

It was six years ago today that episcopal and priestly hands
pushed down upon my head during the rite of ordination. That
memory seems stronger now than it did a year ago. Is it because I am so tired? Does the memory beckon me to thoughts
of better commitments? Or is that memory a self-imposed
mockery of my audacious plans that went awry this year?

The word *priest* becomes more kaleidoscopic in my mind.
Or is my mind becoming more kaleidoscopic as I search for
a meaning for "priest"?

(October 5)
*. . . After all of the plans and ads and work and painting
and washing and greasing and counting and worrying and
spending in this year, I think that the best thing I did at all
was to spend some long hours with a dying human being. Yes,
of course, I did meet some fine people, and I learned a lot of
things about a lot of things; none of it was really a waste. But
I now have to face the* cost *of the American dream . . . and
it's high. I'm not going to ask my family to sink any more
money into* my *problem . . .*

That Tuesday in early August probably changed my life the
most.

The *Los Angeles Times* had just printed a large story on
our efforts, which was picked up by ABC-TV news, and that
in turn led to countless phone calls and letters of interest. I
had been painting at the third car wash (our latest acquisi-
tion) for weeks, while worrying about the other two operations and trying to find a building in which to locate the first
halfway house.

Dead tired, covered with splotches of various metal paints, I answered a phone call from my accountant, who seized the occasion for a recital of the year's financial losses. I listened for several minutes.

After that phone conversation, I don't remember too much until the next day. I know that I asked Jesse to drive me home. I recall going to our bedroom, lying down on the bed, lighting a cigarette, and starting to sob quietly and uncontrollably. The last thing I remember of that day was the thought that I must not completely fall apart.

Jude was there, of course. Frightened, strong, gentle. She told me later that I stared, cried, and slept for several hours. The next morning she demanded that I leave the city for awhile.

"Drive up the coast, take a plane trip, go *anywhere*—just get away from all of this for a time. I'm not kidding around. I'll handle things here."

I went up the coast to Cambria for a week.

(*October 5*)
". . . *If I must choose between saving face or saving my small mind, I'll take the latter. All of this may sound very selfish, but I know what has happened to me in the past year, and that scares me: headaches, tight stomach, sleepless hours, grudging time to my wife and kids, ill humor. I'm sorry, but no thanks.*"

My coastal respite gave me hours and days of visions of the year, and the evidence increased even more upon my return. The pressures increased from both the business and the Foundation, and I sought only to keep myself together. Friends were changing their responses to me as I became "different" to them. The rituals of love expressed to Judy too often became afterthoughts to worries of finances and employees and fund raising. Letters from family and friends echoed concerns about a changing atmosphere in the Jackson home.

I tried to respond to the warnings I heard, but how? I wanted desperately to rekindle the warmth of other days, but how? I must not fall apart.

I gave Lloyd the task of running the business, and I focused my attention on the Foundation. There was at least some hope there.

"Melvin does not actually mind working at the car wash, although, to be absolutely truthful, other opportunities have excited him more. The main thing is, his probation officer is temporarily content.

"After a month or so, he said, he planned to move on to something better. He said he might decide to be a machinist again, adding that he could probably find a job in two or three days if he put his mind to it.

"Tom Jackson is not surprised by Melvin's view, has no illusions to be shattered. 'We're just giving people a chance to get out of jail and get started,' he said. From his experience, none of them are particularly grateful to be working in a car wash. 'If they thought a car wash was the best job in the world then I would think there was something wrong with them.'

"The way Melvin sees it, any man who is in business is in business to make money. If not, he's crazy.

"When Melvin hears about Tom Jackson and Lloyd Wilson, he does not immediately accept the fact that they might be crazy. It is outside his experience that this could be so.

" 'They making a whole lot of money,' he said, shaking his head. 'Just gotta be.' "

(*The* Los Angeles Times, *July 30, 1973*)

I had to make the Foundation work. After weeks of looking, I found a large house in the city, borrowed money from family and friends, and bought Marcliff its first project. Eric and Karol Roth arrived from Ohio to operate the house, and I concentrated on hope. Painting, sanding, and patching continued during the days, while licensing applications occupied too many evening hours. The work was punctuated with continuing reports on the disastrous business outlook, and I isolated myself even more to accomplish the Foundation goal. I knew of nothing else to do.

Suddenly, I had the opportunity to sell one of the businesses to a family in Chicago, and the chance for a large capital gain tempted me strongly. I flew to Chicago and had a long conversation with them at O'Hare Airport—and for the first time in months I felt good inside when I decided not to take their money for a losing operation.

So I flew to Washington for no good reason except to find out if things were as screwed up as the daily papers reported. Yup. Cox, Richardson, and Ruckelshaus had just been canned by Our Leader. Police were on overtime guarding government buildings. Congressmen spoke to me about impeachment, and my cab driver told me that everyone was broke and going nuts.

I flew home.

(October 5)
. . . I have blown a very large wad of money and, as I am the first to admit, there is nothing around us that provides a more specific judgment than that. I don't especially enjoy baring these personal thoughts to all of you, but you have been intimately involved in one way or another—and I think that honesty will untighten my gut at least a bit.

One personal note: I remain convinced that there are one hell of a lot of good people in this world. And excuse the embarrassing words, but I care for each of you very much.

For Paxco, the fears became a reality this past week, and all operations were ceased. There is simply nothing more to do for it, no more assets in my own account to offer, no more corporate ideas to try. I often think of Zorba standing at the foot of his disastrous idea—and then turning to dance. Turning to dance.

For the Marcliff Foundation, the assets are strong in the people involved. Lloyd is taking over as president, the Roths have moved into the house to accept the first residents, and Bob Iles has started a separate project, a sex-education institute for professional counselors. People are giving money and skills and ideas, and Marcliff is becoming soil for innovation, I think.

I realized a short time ago that I would only be an observer here now, that it is time to move on to other places and other people and other hopes.

These past sixteen months came from a whim of hope, an act of independence—and we must accept the ambivalent results. I think of the words of the childhood game: "Go back two steps, you didn't say 'May I.' " And I say: Hell no, I won't go back two steps. There is too much to be found yet, too many good things to be discovered or reclaimed.

That woman I love, those kids I cherish, those friends and family who beckon, those new faces in Ithaca, that old building by the waterfall. I won't take steps back from any or all of that. We can be lovers and laughers and builders and dreamers, even if we don't always say "May I."

Well, my children, what shall I say to you?

I say that I've had a good life, and I've been loved.

I say that my one great hope for you is that you will grow up to feel good about yourselves as human beings.

I say that we will build a home, play in the snow, and dream dreams together.

And I say the words from *The Little Prince* by Antoine de Saint-Exupéry: *"Now here is my secret, a very simple secret: It is only with the heart that one can see rightly; what is essential is invisible to the eye. It is the time you have wasted for your rose that makes your rose so important. You become responsible for what you have loved."*